STEAM LOCOMOTIVES OF BRITISH RAILWAYS

STEAM LOCOMOTIVES OF BRITISH RAILWAYS

H. C. Casserley

Hamlyn Books

London · New York · Sydney · Toronto

A pictorial record originally produced in 1961 by
H. C. Casserley jointly with the late L. L. Asher

First published 1961
Second impression 1963
Third impression 1963
Second edition 1965
Third edition 1973

Published by
The Hamlyn Publishing Group Limited
London · New York · Sydney · Toronto
Astronaut House, Feltham, Middlesex, England

Copyright © H. C. Casserley 1973

ISBN 0 600 02210 2
Printed by Chapel River Press, Andover, Hampshire

Contents

Introduction

The first edition of this book appeared in 1961, not long after the emergence from Swindon of the last new steam engine to be built for British Railways, following the decision to abandon steam in favour of diesel and electric traction. At that time there were some 13,000 steam locomotives still in service, and the original programme provided that they would be gradually phased out by the year 1972. It could hardly then have been envisaged that this plan would be so accelerated that their complete liquidation (apart from three small narrow-gauge engines) would be implemented in little more than half that time, by 1968 in fact, but this nevertheless was what actually happened. So great was B.R.'s obsession with the promotion of the new 'diesel' image of modernisation that a complete ban was placed on the running of steam locomotives over any of its lines, although there were a number in good working order, mainly in private hands, which were quite capable of so doing.

Fortunately this severe edict has now been relaxed to some extent and the pleasure of a steam-hauled special may once again be enjoyed over selected main lines of the British Railways system.

The last edition of this book appeared in 1965, by which time the number of locomotives was down to about 3,000, and during the ensuing three years these too were taken out of service, many of them being quite new with many potential years of good service in them, but all consigned ruthlessly to the scrap-heap in one of the most wasteful exercises ever conceived. Whilst admittedly steam propulsion could never have operated the high-speed 'Inter City' trains of today, there are many secondary services on which steam locomotives could have worked out much of their value. However, this is now history, and re-grettably this record has to be written entirely in the past tense except in so far as the very considerable number of engines which have survived under the preservation movement is concerned.

The scope of the volume carries out the original intention of illustrating all classes of steam locomotives owned by British Railways since its constitution on 1 January, 1948, together with brief notes on the origin and history of each class.

Examples of the varying styles of painting which have been in use since January 1948 are also shown. There are the immediate pre-Nationalisation styles of the four groups; the early variations of British Railways' numbering, when many locomotives were temporarily renumbered in the style of the four owning companies; and the later style with 'British Railways' appearing on the tender or tank sides, in some cases in the type of lettering in use on the appropriate former group. There are also the standard designs of painting, incorporating the lion-and-wheel emblem, which were evolved after a year or two of these temporary styles. They lasted for a good many years, but were superseded in 1957 by a somewhat modified design.

As is generally known, the colours finally adopted, after experiments with shades of blue and light green, were Great Western green for the top-link express engines, and L.N.W.R. black for the intermediates, mixed traffics and passenger tank engines. In 1958 twenty L.M.S. 'Pacifics' were repainted in crimson lake and lined out in yellow and black, the former livery of the L.M.S. company, inherited from the old Midland Railway. Other classes were painted plain black. This comprised mainly the freight and shunting engines, but in practice there was no hard and fast rule as to where the distinction between these and the mixed traffics came. The works of the former Scottish, Northern, Eastern, and Southern companies usually interpreted the passenger style of painting on a far more generous basis than did Crewe, Derby, Swindon and Stratford. The latter group frequently turned out unmistakable passenger classes in unlined black, whereas the former enhanced with added embellishment the appearance of comparatively insignificant classes devoted entirely to shunting.

It would be impractical, even if the required number of photographs was available, to depict every possible variation in every different style of painting which existed during this period. The photographs included have been carefully selected to give as representative a cross-section as possible. With this ideal in view, minor differences, such as varieties of chimney and tender design, are illustrated at least once. In addition, variations in one class which in some way affect a similar class are cross referenced, especially when they involve a departure from the standard practice.

Dimensions, where given, must be taken to apply to the majority of the class, but some individual engines varied in some respects. This frequently happened with cylinder dimensions and boiler pressure.

Lack of space prevents the listing of the numerous names carried by many classes of locomotive, chiefly the express passenger types.

In 1957 the Western Region tried a novel experiment in restoring their celebrated engine *City of Truro*, which had been housed in York Museum for over twenty-five years, to working order and repainting it in its old G.W.R. livery. In this condition it was used mainly to work enthusiasts' special trains. But when not so engaged it was also frequently employed in ordinary light passenger service. It has now been permanently retired and is in Swindon Museum. This admirable example was subsequently followed in Scotland, where two preserved engines, the Caledonian single No. 123 and the Highland 'Jones Goods' No. 103, were once more put into working order, together with a North British 'Glen' and the last G.N.S.R. 4-4-0 'Gordon Highlander'; all four were also restored to their pre-grouping liveries. Similarly, in 1959 the London Midland Region completely renovated the first of the famous Deeley compounds, which had been kept at Crewe since its withdrawal in 1951. It was restored to all the glory of its former Midland crimson lake, and also steamed for passenger working on special occasions. It was subsequently placed in the Clapham Museum, together with many other engines, until this was closed in April 1973, most of the exhibits being moved to York.

The growth of the preservation movement during the last ten years or so, through numerous societies, organisations, groups and individuals, is too well known to need further comment here, beyond mentioning that there are now several hundred steam locomotives scattered round the country, not all accessible to public view. Many, however, can be seen either as static exhibits in museums or at other locations, and there is also a considerable number of preserved railways with lengths of line varying from a few hundred yards to several miles where steam trains are operated, mainly at weekends during the summer months for the benefit of enthusiasts.

Mention of main line engines which have been saved from the scrap-heap is made in the appropriate section, although this may not be quite complete, as there are at the time of writing still some two hundred engines lying derelict in the yards at Barry, in South Wales, owned by the firm of Woodhams. After the ravages of weather over several years they are naturally in sorry condition, but even now groups of enthusiasts are investigating the better ones, and several more may yet be restored to their former glory, an extensive project apart from the not inconsiderable purchase price at scrap values. For details of the actual location of preserved engines and lines readers must be referred to the section at the end of the book and the map on the back endpaper.

Most of the photographs were taken by the author. Others are duly credited where the authorship is known, but a few are from unidentified sources.

Class List–Historical Data
List of Illustrations

THE GREAT WESTERN GROUP

The Great Western Group

At Nationalisation on 1 January, 1948, the Great Western Railway possessed 3,857 steam locomotives of some sixty main classes, many of which embraced several varieties of major and minor importance. It is endeavoured to provide typical illustrations of each class, showing any main variations which result in a marked difference to the external appearance of the locomotive, although it is not practicable to depict every possible variation which may be found in each class.

Upon Nationalisation, when the need for renumbering most of the locomotive stock of the four groups into one comprehensive numbering scheme soon became apparent and in order to avoid confusion through duplication, it was decided to increase the numbers of the L.M.S., L.N.E.R. and Southern by an appropriate number of thousands, as described in the introductory notes to the sections dealing with those three lines, and to leave the Great Western numbers as they were. This decision was mainly or entirely governed by the fact that, alone of the four groups, the G.W.R. still used brass number-plates on its engines. The other three groups had always used painted numbers and it was considered more economical to leave the Great Western number-plates as they were without alteration. Not only this, but all locomotives built since 1948 to G.W.R. designs – and the last of them only appeared as recently as 1956 – have been fitted with the Swindon style of number-plate and consequently they stand alone in not conforming to British Railways' standard practice in this respect. Whilst these number-plates are of handsome design with a most pleasing style of figures, unlike the modern Gill Sans type, they nevertheless have the disadvantage that, when they are allowed to become dirty, as is too often unfortunately the case, they are almost unreadable at any distance or in a bad light.

Because of the Great Western's somewhat peculiar method of numbering its modern standard designs, it is not easy to enumerate the various classes in strict numerical order, as the various batches of each type become interspersed with one another. This will become more clear when it is explained that the numbering method was to keep, as far as possible, the *second* numeral in each four-figure number (i.e. the hundreds) constant for any one class. For example, the final outside-cylindered 2-6-0's were Nos. 4300-4399, followed by 5300-5399, 6300-6399, and so on. The numerous standard 0-6-0PT's, which began with 5700-5799, eventually filled up all the available 700 numbers up to 9799, and then went back to 3700-3799; further additions had to go into the 600

11

series, starting with 3600–3699, and later followed by other batches. Whether this system had any real advantage was questionable, as some of the somewhat similar numbers, for example No. 5383 and No. 6383, were liable to become a little confusing and difficult to distinguish at times, even to those with a good memory for numbers. This system, however, was perpetuated to the end, the final new construction of G.W.R.-type engines following the old tradition by being turned out as Nos. 9400–9499, then 8400–8499, and a final ten locomotives, which did not appear until 1956, had to take the numbers 3400–3409, the next lowest available '400' series not already occupied by other classes.

With a few exceptions, therefore, numbers of Great Western engines were unaffected after Nationalisation. The exceptions were the result of a minor renumbering scheme which the Great Western itself started in 1946. This concerned only a few small groups of engines from the absorbed South Wales lines which had scattered numbers and were being brought together for the sake of convenience. The scheme was gradually completed as the engines went through the works, and details are given when dealing with the respective classes. Later another small renumbering involving engines 9300–9319 was undertaken, under which they followed earlier locomotives of the same class as Nos. 7322–7341.

It should be mentioned that for a short time after Nationalisation some engines appeared with a painted 'W' above the number plate, part of a temporary scheme under which each of the four groups retained their existing numbers, with the addition of a prefix letter, but this was soon dropped when the general renumbering scheme was inaugurated.

For the first years after Nationalisation the production of new engines of Great Western design already on order proceeded, producing the appearance of many new examples of established classes such as 'Castles', 'Halls', 2–6–2T's, standard 0–6–0PT's, and others, whilst an entirely new design of 0–6–0PT, with outside cylinders and Walschaerts valve gear, a startling innovation for the Great Western, appeared in 1949. Only ten engines, however, were built, Nos. 1500–1509. Another new design, if it could be called such, also made its appearance in the same year in the form of a light 0–6–0PT, No. 1600, built to replace much older but very similar engines, dating back to the turn of the century, which were being withdrawn. In all, seventy engines of the new modernised design were built, the last only in 1955, but even so there were still at the close of 1957 a few of the original ones left in service.

The Great Western had, during the last fifty years or so of its existence, developed a very high degree of standardisation, and the products of Swindon bore a marked stamp of individuality, which could not possibly be mistaken.

Twice in the course of our locomotive history, Great Western engines came off better than those of any other railway: firstly at the grouping of 1923, when the status of the G.W.R. was practically untouched, and then after Nationalisation when the Great Western held its own and stood apart in its own traditional way. Even its livery remained unchanged, fortunate as far as Great Western engines were concerned, for there is no doubt that the Swindon dark green was particularly suited to its own locomotives. For some reason it seemed to ill become many engines of other railways, particularly those of the L.M.S. to which it was applied, the reason probably being the absence of brass-work, found on G.W.R. locomotives, which it needed to be set off to its best advantage.

During the last years of steam, withdrawal of G.W.R. types proceeded so rapidly that by 1967 all had become extinct with the exception of Nos. 7–9, the three Vale of Rheidol narrow-gauge locomotives. These were the last steam engines to remain in service on the Nationalised British Railways system. It is of more than passing interest to note that one of them, No. 9, was actually of pre-grouping origin.

Great Western type engines have fared exceedingly well under the various preservation schemes promoted during the last few years by sundry organisations, at least fifty having been saved from the breakers, with still further possibilities from Barry scrap-yard, where a number of such engines remain in 1973. Most of those preserved are of post-grouping construction, but built to G.W.R. design. Indeed there are far more engines of the Great Western type still in existence than of any other pre-grouping railway.

Class List–Historical Data
List of Illustrations

1

0–4–0ST acquired from Ystalyfera Tin Works in 1948. Named *Hercules*. Built by Peckett & Sons in 1900 (Works No. 810) and attached to British Railways service stock. Scrapped in 1954. **p. 117**

3

Corris Railway 0–4–2ST, built in 1878 by Falcon Engine Co. to 2′3″ gauge. Sold in 1951 to the Tal-y-Llyn Railway and now running as No. 3 *Sir Haydn* on that line. **p. 117**

4

0–4–2ST, built by Kerr Stuart in 1921 for the Corris Railway. Sold in 1951 to the Tal-y-Llyn Railway and now running on that line as No. 4 *Edward Thomas*. This engine and the previous one were withdrawn from British Railways' stock in 1948 on the complete closure of the Corris Railway. They possess the unique record of having carried the same numbers, 3 and 4, under four successive ownerships: Corris Railway, Great Western Railway, British Railways and Tal-y-Llyn Railway. **p. 118**

5, 6

Stroudley 0–6–0T's, 'Terrier' class acquired by the G.W.R. in 1940 from the Weston, Clevedon and Portishead Railway which was closed in that year. They were built at Brighton in 1877 and 1875 respectively and were originally L.B. & S.C.R. Nos. 43 and 53. No. 6 (an unnamed engine) was withdrawn in January 1948, but No. 5 *Portishead* lasted until 1954. **p. 118**

7–9

Vale of Rheidol 2–6–2T's with 1′11½″ gauge No. 9 (numbered 1213 until March 1949) was one of the original Vale of Rheidol engines of 1902. Nos. 7

and 8 were built by the Great Western in 1923 and are identical to the original. In 1956 all these engines were painted green and named respectively *Owain Glyndwr, Llywelyn* and *Prince of Wales,* the latter being the engine's name before the 1923 G.W.R. takeover. The only steam locomotives now operated by B.R. (summer service). **p. 119**

28, 29

0–6–0PT's acquired from the Cleobury, Mortimer and Ditton Priors Light Railway. Originally built in 1905 as 0–6–0ST's with 3'6" driving wheels. No. 28 was withdrawn in 1953 and No. 29 in 1954. **p. 119**

30, 31, 32, 34, 46

Rhymney Railway 0–6–2T's, class R, with 4'6" driving wheels. All were taken out of service in 1951. **p. 120**

33, 47, 51

0–6–2T's with 4'6" driving wheels. Built in 1904 for the Rhymney Railway as class M. No. 47 was rebuilt with a Great Western taper boiler, the others retaining their original boilers until their withdrawal in 1951. **p. 120**

35–44

Rhymney 0–6–2T's, class R1, with 4'6" driving wheels, built in 1921. Nos. 39, 40 and 44 were rebuilt with G.W.R. taper boilers. All were scrapped between 1953 and 1958. **p. 121**

52–75

Rhymney 0–6–2T's, class A, driving wheels 4'4½", built 1910–18. Some were rebuilt with Great Western boilers; all were taken out of service by 1955.

p. 122

76–83

0–6–2T's of the Rhymney Railway, classes P and P1, with 5'0" wheels and fitted with vacuum brake for working passenger trains. Built 1909–21; later rebuilt with Great Western boilers and all scrapped by 1955. **p. 123**

15

90–92

Rhymney Railway 0–6–0T's, class S1, built in 1920. No. 91 carried the number 605 until March 1948; the other two (late 604 and 606) had been renumbered in 1947. All were scrapped in 1954. **p. 123**

93–96

Class S 0–6–0T's of the Rhymney Railway, built in 1908. All were later rebuilt with G.W.R. boilers. They were later renumbered from 608–611. No. 610 was renumbered 95 in September 1948, while No. 96 did not receive its new number until December 1949. They were all taken out of service in 1953 and 1954. **p. 124**

155

Cardiff Railway 0–6–2T, a survivor of three engines built in 1908. Later rebuilt with a Great Western boiler and scrapped in 1953. **p. 125**

184

0–6–2T of the Port Talbot Railway. The only surviving locomotive of a batch of ten built in 1898. It was rebuilt with a G.W.R. boiler and finally withdrawn in 1948. **p. 125**

190

Alexandra Docks 0–6–2ST with outside cylinders. Originally one of a class of three engines built in 1908, it was taken out of service in 1948. **p. 126**

193–195

Taff Vale Railway 0–6–0T's with coned boilers and 5'3" driving wheels. They were built in 1884 for working the Pwllyrehebog Incline, but were withdrawn in 1951 when working over this incline was discontinued. Nos. 193 and 195 were sold out of service and No. 194 was scrapped. Formerly numbered 792–794, they were renumbered in 1948-9. **p. 126**

198, 212/3, 231/8, 240/6/8, 258/9, 261–3/5/7–72/4/7

Barry Railway 0–6–2T's, the survivors of a numerous class built between 1888 and 1900, with 4'3" driving wheels. The last of the class was withdrawn from regular service in 1951, but one or two had a longer lease of life, being retained as works shunters at Swindon before being broken up. **p. 127**

359

Hilda, 0–6–0ST acquired from the Llanelly and Mynydd Mawr Railway. Built in 1917 and scrapped in 1954. **p. 127**

200–211, 215–220, 236, 278–299

Taff Vale Railway 0–6–2T's, class O4, built between 1907 and 1910 with 4'6½" driving wheels. Some of the class were fitted with G.W.R. boilers; all were scrapped by 1955. Those numbered between 200 and 220 formerly carried numbers in the 300s and 400s, and several of these did not receive their new numbers until 1948–9. In one or two instances the engines were scrapped without carrying their newly allocated numbers. **p. 128**

303–9, 312/6, 322, 335/7, 343–9, 351/2/6/7, 360–2/4–8, 370–391, 393/4/7–9

Taff Vale 0–6–2T's, built 1914–21 with 5'6" wheels, and designated class A by the parent company. They were vacuum fitted for passenger work. All were rebuilt with Great Western boilers. Withdrawals commenced in 1955 and the last was scrapped in 1958. **p. 129**

410, 411

Taff Vale 0–6–2T's, class O3. Built in 1904 and both taken out of service in 1948. **p. 130**

431–436

Brecon & Merthyr Railway 0–6–2T's with 5'0" wheels, built between 1915 and 1920. Once numbered 1372–1375, 1668 and 1670, they became Nos. 431–6 between 1947 and 1949. Some had been rebuilt with Swindon boilers; all were scrapped between 1951 and 1954. **p. 130**

421–428

Brecon & Merthyr Railway 4'6" 0–6–2T's, built 1910–14. They were formerly numbered 11, 21, 332, 504, 698, 888, 1084 and 1113. Only Nos. 422/5/6/8 actually carried their allocated numbers. Some of the class were later fitted with G.W.R. boilers. No. 1084 (allocated 427) was scrapped in 1947 and consequently did not come into British Railways' stock, while the remainder were withdrawn between 1948 and 1951. **p. 131**

666, 667

Alexandra Docks 0–6–0T's with outside cylinders. These two locomotives were a War Department type of engine and were originally numbered R.O.D. 604 and 602. They were scrapped in 1955 and 1954 respectively. **p. 132**

680

Alexandra Docks 0–6–0ST, built by Peckett's in 1886 and scrapped in 1948.

p. 132

681–684

Cardiff Railway 0–6–0PT's, originally built as saddle tanks in 1920 and scrapped 1954–5. **p. 133**

803

Llanelly & Mynydd Mawr 0–6–0T, built in 1911 and formerly named *Ravelston.* This locomotive was withdrawn in 1951. **p. 133**

783, 784

Barry Railway 0–6–0T's, both built in 1890 and taken out of service in 1948 and 1949 respectively. **p. 134**

822, 823

Welshpool and Llanfair Railway 0–6–0T's, built in 1902 to 2′6½″ gauge. Originally named *The Earl* and *Countess*, the name plates were removed about 1952. The line was finally closed in November 1956. Latterly only one engine, No. 822, had been in use. The line was reopened in 1963 under private ownership, and the two locomotives, which had been retained, are now in service again as Welshpool and Llanfair Nos. 1 and 2. **p. 135**

844/9, 855, 864, 873, 887, 892–6

Cambrian Railway 0–6–0's built between 1908 and 1919 and all withdrawn by 1954. **p. 135**

1000–1029

Hawksworth 2-cylinder 4–6–0's, 6′3″ wheels and 280 lbs. pressure, built 1945–7. The class was named after counties. No. 1000 was built with a double blast pipe and chimney and later some others were similarly fitted. All withdrawn 1962–4. **pp. 136–7**

1101–1106

0–4–0T dock shunters with 3′9½″ wheels, built in 1926. All were withdrawn early in 1960. **p. 137**

1140

Swansea Harbour Trust 0–4–0ST built by Andrew Barclay in 1905. This engine was numbered 701 until June 1948. It was scrapped in 1958.　　**p. 138**

1141

Swansea Harbour Trust 0–4–0ST built by Peckett's in 1906. Numbered 929 until March 1948, it was finally scrapped in 1952.　　**p. 138**

1142

Swansea Harbour Trust 0–4–0ST built by Hudswell Clarke in 1911. Until November 1948, this locomotive was numbered 943. Scrapped in 1959.　　**p. 139**

1143

Swansea Harbour Trust 0–4–0ST built by Peckett's in 1908 and numbered 968 until February 1949. Withdrawn in 1961.　　**p. 139**

1144

Swansea Harbour Trust 0–4–0ST built by Hawthorn Leslie in 1909. Numbered 974 until September 1948. Withdrawn early in 1960.　　**p. 140**

1145

Swansea Harbour Trust 0–4–0ST built by Peckett's in 1918. Numbered 1098 until January 1950. Scrapped in 1959.　　**p. 140**

1146, 1147

Swansea Harbour Trust 0–6–0ST's built between 1912 and 1913 by Peckett's. They were numbered 1085/6 until 1949 and were both scrapped two years later.
p. 141

1150–1152

Powlesland & Mason 0–4–0ST's built by Peckett's in 1912, 1913 and 1916. The three engines were numbered 696 (until December 1951), 779 (until October 1950) and 935 (until June 1950). No. 1150 was withdrawn in 1952, No. 1151 in 1963 and No. 1152 in 1962.　　**p. 141**

1153

Powlesland & Mason 0–4–0ST built in 1903 by Hawthorn Leslie. It was originally named *Dorothy* and numbered 942 until November 1949. The engine was taken out of service in 1955. **p. 142**

1196, 1197

Cambrian 2–4–0T's built in 1866 and withdrawn in 1948. **p. 142**

1205, 1206

Alexandra Docks 2–6–2T's built 1920. No. 1205 was scrapped in 1951 and No. 1206 in 1956. **p. 143**

1308

2–4–0T, *Lady Margaret*, built in 1902 for the Liskeard & Looe Railway. It was acquired by the Great Western when they took over that line in 1909 and was finally scrapped in 1948. **p. 143**

1331

0–6–0ST built by Fox Walker in 1877 and acquired by the G.W.R. in 1886 from the Whitland & Cardigan Railway. It was withdrawn in 1950. **p. 144**

1334–1336

Midland & South Western Junction Railway 2–4–0's built in 1894. They had 5'6" wheels and were latterly superheated by the Great Western. The first two of the class were taken out of service in 1952, but No. 1336 lasted until 1954.

p. 144

1338

Cardiff Railway 0–4–0ST built by Kitson's in 1898, which ran until 1963, when it was finally withdrawn. It has been preserved. **p. 145**

1358

Port Talbot Railway 0–8–2T, one of three engines built by Sharp, Stewart in 1901. Scrapped in 1948, the other two having been withdrawn in 1926 and 1935.

p. 145

1361–1365

0–6–0ST dock shunters built in 1910 with 3'8" wheels and outside cylinders. All withdrawn 1961–2. No. 1363 has been preserved.   **p. 146**

1366–1371

0–6–0PT dock shunters with 3'8" wheels and outside cylinders, built 1934. Nos. 1367–1369 were withdrawn from the former Southern Railway Wenford Bridge branch in Cornwall in late 1964. No. 1369 has been preserved.   **p. 146**

1400–1474

Collett 0–4–2T's built 1932–6. They were fitted with pull-and-push apparatus for rail motor work. Until 1946 they were numbered 4800–4874. Withdrawal began in 1956 and was completed in 1964. Nos. 1420, 1442, 1450 and 1466 have been preserved.   **p. 147**

1500–1509

Hawksworth heavy 0–6–0PT's with outside cylinders, built 1949. Some were sold to the National Coal Board and the remainder were withdrawn by early 1964. No 1501 has been preserved.   **p. 148**

1600–1669

Light 0–6–0PT's with 4'1½" wheels, built 1949–55, to replace old Dean 0–6–0PT's of somewhat similar design. Scrapping began in 1959 and was completed by 1966. No. 1638 has been preserved.   **p. 148**

906, 907, 1531/2/8/42, 1705/6/9, 1713/5, 1720/6, 1730/1, 1742/5/7/9, 1752–4/8, 1760/2/4/9, 1773, 1780/2/9, 1835, 1855/8, 1861–3/7, 1870/8, 1884/8/9, 1891/4/6/7, 1900, 2702/4/6–9, 2712–7/9, 2721/2/4/8, 2730/4/8/9, 2743–6/8/9, 2751/2/4–7, 2760/1/4/7/9, 2771/2/4/6, 2780/1/5 7/9–95/7/9

4'7½" 0–6–0PT's of various classes, with minor differences, built at Swindon and Wolverhampton between 1879 and 1901. Originally constructed as saddle tanks, the survivors had been gradually rebuilt over a long period with the square pannier type. No. 1715 had been sold to the Neath & Brecon Railway in 1914 and came back to the Great Western under its original number at the grouping. No. 2756 had similarly been the property of the Rhondda & Swansea Bay Railway. All these engines had been scrapped by 1951.   **p. 149**

992, 1903/7/9, 1912/7/9, 1925, 1930/5, 1941/3/5/9, 1957, 1964/5/7–9, 1973/9, 1989, 1990/1/3/6, 2000–2/4/6–14/6–9, 2021–3/5–7/9–35/7–40/2–5/7/8, 2050–6/9–61/3–73/5/6/9, 2080–83/5/6/8–99, 2100–2/4/6–15/7, 2121–4/6/7/9–32/4–8, 2140/1/4/6–8, 2150–6/9, 2160, 2181–90

0–6–0PT's of various classes with minor differences, with 4'1½" wheels, built between 1875 and 1905 at Swindon and Wolverhampton. They were all originally constructed as saddle tanks, and all of the survivors, except Nos. 1925 and 2007, had been rebuilt as pannier tanks. These two locomotives retained the round saddle until withdrawn in 1951 and 1949 respectively. No. 2048 was also a saddle tank until 1948 when it was rebuilt to pannier design. Nos. 2181–2190 initially belonged to the 2021–2160 series, but in 1939–40 they were given increased braking power and renumbered. Apart from this there was no alteration. The last of the class was withdrawn in 1959.　　　　**pp. 150–1**

2162, 2164–2168, 2198

Burry Port & Gwendraeth Valley Railway 0–6–0T's, built 1910–19 and all scrapped by 1956 with the exception of No. 2198, which lasted until 1959.
　　　　p. 152

2176

Burry Port & Gwendraeth Valley Railway 0–6–0ST, built in 1907 when it was named *Pembrey*. It was taken out of service in 1955.　　**p. 153**

2192, 2193

Burry Port & Gwendraeth Valley Railway 0–6–0ST's, built in 1900–1 and scrapped in 1951–2.　　　　**p. 153**

2194, 2195

Burry Port & Gwendraeth Valley Railway 0–6–0ST's built between 1903 and 1905. No. 2194 was named *Kidwelly*, while at one time No. 2195 bore the name *Cwm Mawr*. Both were scrapped in 1953.　　　　**p. 154**

2196

Burry Port & Gwendraeth Valley Railway 0–6–0ST, built in 1906 and named *Gwendraeth*. Scrapped in 1956.　　　　**p. 154**

2197

Burry Port & Gwendraeth Valley Railway 0–6–0T, built in 1909 and named *Pioneer*. It was withdrawn in 1955.　　　　**p. 155**

2322/3/7, 2339, 2340/3/9–51/4/6, 2383/5/6, 2401/7–9, 2411/4, 2426, 2431, 2444/5/9, 2452/8, 2460/2/4/8, 2474, 2482–4, 2513/5/6, 2523, 2532/4/7/8, 2541/3, 2551/6, 2568–70/2/3/8/9

Dean 0–6–0's built between 1883 and 1899. The survivors were part of a class of 260 locomotives, exclusive of a further 20 which were built with outside frames. Many of the class were loaned to the Government during both World Wars for active service abroad. The last survivor, No. 2538, was withdrawn in 1957, but No. 2516 has been preserved in Swindon Museum. **p. 156**

2200–2299, 3200–3219

Collett 0–6–0's built between 1930 and 1948. Withdrawal began in 1958 and was completed in 1965. No. 3205 has been preserved. **p. 157**

2612, 2620/3, 2643, 2651/5/6, 2662/5/7/9, 2680

2–6–0 freight locomotives with outside frames and inside cylinders designed by William Dean. They were originally a class of 81 engines, built between 1899 and 1902, and generally went by the nickname of 'Aberdares'. The last of the class was scrapped in 1949. **p. 155**

2800–2899, 3800–66

Churchward 2–8–0 2-cylinder freight engines, built 1903–19, and perpetuated by Collett with slight modifications (No. 2884 onwards) from 1938–42. Between 1946 and 1949 several of the class were converted to oil burners and during this period they were renumbered temporarily in the 4800s, reverting to their original numbers on reconversion to coal burning. The locomotives concerned were as follows (temporary numbers in brackets):

2832 (4806)	2834 (4808)	2839 (4804)	2845 (4809)
2847 (4811)	2848 (4807)	2849 (4803)	2853 (4810)
2854 (4801)	2862 (4802)	2863 (4805)	2872 (4800)
2888 (4850)	3813 (4855)	3818 (4852)	3820 (4856)
3831 (4857)	3837 (4854)	3839 (4853)	3865 (4851)

Scrapping of the earlier engines commenced in 1958 and was completed in 1966. Nos. 2818 and 2857 have been preserved. **pp. 158–9**

3002/4–6, 3008–3044, 3046–9

Robinson's design of 2–8–0 for the Great Central Railway, of which large numbers were constructed for the War Department during the First World War. The Great Western acquired 100 of the locomotives between 1919 and 1921. 45 of the class remained in 1948, but since then the remainder have been scrapped, the last in 1958. **p. 159**

2902/3/5/6/8, 2912/3/5/6, 2920/4, 2926–2955, 2979–81, 2987–9

Churchward 2-cylinder 4–6–0's, wheel diameter $6'8\frac{1}{2}''$, built between 1902 and 1913. Originally a class of 77 engines numbered 2900–2955, 2971–2990 and 2998. Nos. 2971/2, 2979–2990 were constructed as 'Atlantics' and later converted to 4–6–0's. Successive batches were named after ladies, saints, courts, and sundry names associated with Sir Walter Scott's novels, but the whole class was generally known as 'Saints'. No. 2925 *Saint Martin* was rebuilt in 1924 with '0'' wheels and renumbered 4900, becoming the prototype of the 'Hall' class. Scrapping commenced in 1931 and the last survivor, No. 2920 *Saint David*, was withdrawn in 1953.   **pp. 160–1**

3100–3104

2–6–2T's with $5'3''$ wheels, reconstructed in 1938–9 from Churchward engines with $5'8''$ wheels originally built in 1907. Their former numbers were 3173, 3156, 3181, 3155 and 3179. All were withdrawn between 1957 and 1959.

p. 162

3150/1/3/4/7–61/3/4/5/7–72/4–8, 3180/2–90

Churchward 2–6–2T's, driving wheels $5'8''$, built between 1906 and 1908. Five of these locomotives were rebuilt into the '3100' class in 1938–9 (see above). The last to survive was No. 3170, which was scrapped in 1958.   **p. 162**

4100–4179, 5101–14/7/9, 5121/2/5/7–32/4–44/6–8/50–99

Churchward 2–6–2T's with $5'8''$ wheels, built 1903–6, and perpetuated by Collett between 1929 and 1949. There were originally 40 engines of the earlier series, at first numbered 3100 and 3111–3149, but later altered to 5100 and 5111–5149. The prototype was constructed in 1903. Of these, ten were reconstructed in 1938–9 with $5'6''$ wheels and renumbered 8100–8109 (see below). The last survivor, 5148, went in 1964. Withdrawal of the later locomotives (4100–4179, 5101–5110 and 5150–5199) commenced in 1957 and was completed in 1965. Nos. 4141 and 5164 have been preserved.   **p. 163**

6100–6169

Collett 2–6–2T's with $5'8''$ wheels, similar to the 4100 class but with 225 lbs. pressure instead of 200 lbs. Built 1931–5. No. 6100 withdrawn in 1958, the others by 1965. No. 6106 has been preserved.   **p. 163**

8100–8109

2–6–2T's with $5'6''$ wheels, reconstructed in 1938–9 by Collett from $5'8''$ engines originally built 1903–6 (see above) from a design by Churchward. Their former numbers were respectively: 5100, 5123, 5118, 5145, 5124, 5126, 5120, 5116, 5133 and 5115. All withdrawn between 1957 and 1965.   **p. 162**

3335, 3341, 3363/4/6, 3376/7/9, 3382/3/6, 3391/3/5/6, 3400/1/6–8, 3417–9, 3421/6, 3430–2/8, 3440–3455

Dean and Churchward 5'8" 4–4–0's with outside frames, built between 1899 and 1910. The majority of the class carried miscellaneous names, the last 15, Nos. 3441–3455, being named after birds. The class was generally known as 'Bulldogs', the name carried by No. 3311, one of the original locomotives. No. 3335 was the only survivor of the earlier series, which had curved frames over the driving wheels, the later ones having straight frames. The last of the class was withdrawn in 1951.   **pp. 164–5**

3440

Churchward 6'8½" 4–4–0 express engine, one of a series of 20 constructed in 1901–3. *City of Truro* achieved world fame in 1904 by being the first engine officially recorded as having attained a speed of over 100 miles per hour. On withdrawal in 1931 it was sent to York Museum for preservation, but early in 1957 it was renovated and put into service once more, mainly for working enthusiasts' specials, but when not so employed it ran in ordinary service. It has been restored to the old G.W.R. livery of the 1903 period and has reverted to its original number of 3440. From 1912 until 1957 this locomotive carried the number 3717. It was again withdrawn in 1962 and now rests in Swindon Museum with its 3717 number.   **p. 165**

3561/2, 3582/5/6/8/9, 3592/7/9

The survivors of a once numerous class of 2–4–0T's, the later series, to which the remaining engines belonged, having been built in 1894–9. All were taken out of service by 1949.   **p. 166**

3574/5/7

The remaining locomotives of a large class of 0–4–2T's, forerunners of the present 1400 and 5800 classes. These were constructed between 1895 and 1897, and were all withdrawn by 1949.   **p. 166**

3600–3799, 4600–4699, 5700–5799, 6700–6779, 7700–7799, 8700–99, 9600–9682, 9700–9799

Collett's standard 0–6–0PT's with 4'7½" wheels. The 863 engines of this type, built 1929–49, constituted the largest class in the country. There were a few

25

detailed variations, but all were in the main of one uniform design. The principal deviations from the standard were found in engines 9700–9711, which were fitted with condensing apparatus for working through the Metropolitan line tunnels in the London area. Cab design also underwent a change with the later-built ones. Nos. 6700–6779 were fitted with steam brakes only and confined to shunting duties, mainly in the South Wales division. The other engines, although their principal functions were shunting and shorthaul freight trains, were vacuum fitted and were often to be found working passenger trains. The order of construction was: 5700–5799, 6700–6749, 7700–7799, 9700 (first numbered 8700), 8701–8799, 8700, 9701–9799, 3700–3799, 3600–3699, 4600–4699, 9600–9661, 6750–6759, 9662–9682, 6760–6779. Withdrawal began in 1956 and was completed in 1966. Nos. 3650 and 9642 have been preserved. Thirteen were sold to London Transport from 1956 onwards, some being used until 1971, and have been acquired for preservation. **pp. 167–9**

4003/4/7, 4012/3/5/7–23/5/6/8, 4030/1/3–6/8–62

Churchward 4-cylinder 4–6–0's, 6'8½" wheels, built between 1906 and 1923. A class of originally 73 locomotives numbered 4000–4072. No. 4000 was initially constructed as an 'Atlantic' and converted later to a 4–6–0. Successive batches were named after stars, knights, kings (later renamed monarchs), queens, princes, princesses, and abbeys, but the whole class was generally known under the generic name of 'Stars'. Nos. 4000, 4009, 4016, 4032, 4037 and 4063–4072 were later rebuilt as 'Castles' (see below). Withdrawal of the remainder commenced in 1932 and the last survivor in traffic was No. 4056, withdrawn in October 1957. No. 4003 *Lode Star* is preserved in Swindon Museum. **pp. 170–1**

100A1, 111, 4000, 4016, 4032, 4037, 4073–4099, 5000–5099, 7000–7037

Collett 4-cylinder 4–6–0's with 6'8½" wheels, a development of Churchward's 'Star' class. The majority of them were named after castles, and although there were some deviations from this general rule, the class as a whole was known as 'Castles'. Nos. 4073–4099, 5000–5082, 5093–5099 and 7000–7037 were built new at varying periods between 1923 and 1950, but the rest are rebuilds. Nos. 4000, 4009, 4016, 4032 and 4037 were rebuilt from 'Star' to 'Castle' class between 1925 and 1929. No. 4009 *Shooting Star* was subsequently renumbered and renamed 100A1 *Lloyds* in 1936. Nos. 5083–5092 were formerly 'Star' class locomotives Nos. 4063–4072, which were named after abbeys, and reconstructed in 1937–40 retaining their 'Abbey' names. The remaining engine, No. 111, was a reconstruction of the Great Western's only 'Pacific', *The Great Bear*, which was converted from 4–6–2 to 4–6–0 in 1924. It retained its old number 111, but was renamed *Viscount Churchill*. A certain amount of renaming took place amongst the class; the name *Ogmore Castle* was carried by no less than three engines: first on No. 5080 which later became *Defiant*, then on No. 7007 which was subsequently re-

26

named *Great Western*, and finally on the new No. 7035 built in 1950. No. 7037 was named *Swindon* to commemorate the fact that it was the last express passenger engine of G.W.R. design to be built at the famous works. In February 1952, No. 4082 *Windsor Castle* and No. 7013 *Bristol Castle* exchanged names and numbers, as it was desired that the funeral train conveying the late King George VI on his last journey to Windsor should be hauled by a locomotive bearing an appropriate name. The original No. 4082, which King George had once driven on a visit to Swindon, was unfortunately not in suitable condition at the time. The two locomotives remained under their changed identities. Withdrawal began in 1959 and was completed in 1965. Nos. 4073, 4079, 5051, 7027 and 7029 have been preserved. **pp. 171–3**

6000–6029

'King' class 4-cylinder 4–6–0's, with 6'6" wheels and 250 lbs. pressure, built by Collett from 1927 to 1930. These engines remained the Great Western's most powerful passenger engines until the end of its existence. Unlike the other three groups the G.W.R. never adopted the 'Pacific' type of locomotive for top-link work, after its experiment with *The Great Bear* in 1908. All were latterly fitted with double-blast pipes and chimneys. The whole class was withdrawn from traffic in 1962, but Nos. 6000 and 6024 have been preserved. **p. 174**

4303, 4318, 4320/6, 4337, 4353/8, 4365, 4375/7, 4381/6, 5300/2/3/5–7/9–28, 5330–41/3–51/3/5–62/4/5/7–82/4–6/8, 5390–2/4–9, 6300–6314, 6316–6399, 7300–7321, 8393, 9300–19

Churchward mixed traffic 2–6–0's, with 5'8" wheels, built between 1911 and 1932. The class originally ran complete from 4300–4399, 5300–5399, 6300–6399, 7300–7321 and 9300–9319. In 1928 most of the 5300 series underwent slight modifications and were given corresponding numbers in the 8300s. From 1944 onwards these gradually reverted to their original 5300 numbers and all had been so altered by January 1948, with the exception of No. 8393, which ran with this number until September 1948, when it eventually reverted to No. 5393. Nos. 9300–9319 were latterly renumbered 7322–7341. All withdrawn by 1964. No. 5322 has been preserved. **p. 175**

4200/1/3/6–8, 4211–5/7/8, 4221–33/5–8, 4241–3/6–8, 4250–4299, 5200–5264

Churchward 2–8–0T's, 4'7½" wheels, for heavy short-haul mineral traffic, built 1910–40. In all, 205 engines were constructed to this design: Nos. 4200–4299 and 5200–5294 between 1910 and 1930, and a final 10 in 1940. In 1934, Nos. 5275–5294 were reconstructed as 2–8–2T's and renumbered 7200–7219, while in 1935–6 Nos. 5255–5274 were similarly treated and became Nos. 7220–7239.

These were followed in 1937 by 14 more reconstructions from the earlier loco-motives, which were duly renumbered 7240–7253, their original numbers having been 4239, 4220, 4202, 4204, 4216, 4205, 4234, 4244, 4249, 4209, 4219, 4240, 4210 and 4425 respectively. Rather strangely, 10 further engines were built in 1940 as 2–8–0T's, numbered 5255–5264, but they were, of course, entirely different engines from those which at first bore these numbers, and which were then 2–8–2T's, Nos. 7220–7229. Withdrawal began in 1959 and was completed by 1965. There were still a few at Barry in 1973, of which No. 5224 at least may be preserved.

p. 176

7200–7253

Collett 2–8–2T's, rebuilt from Churchward 2–8–0T's, details of which are given above. All withdrawn between 1962 and 1965. No. 7202 has been preserved.

p. 177

4400–4410

2–6–2T's with $4'1\frac{1}{2}''$ driving wheels, designed by Churchward for steeply graded branch lines. Built in 1904–6, their usual spheres of activity were on the Prince-town, Liskeard and Looe, Much Wenlock and Tondu branches. All of the class were scrapped between 1949 and 1955.

p. 178

4500–4599, 5500–5574

Churchward and Collett 2–6–2T's, with $4'7\frac{1}{2}''$ wheels, built between 1906 and 1929. They were built for working branch lines and for general cross-country work. Nos. 4575 onwards were of a modified design with increased water capacity. All withdrawn between 1950 and 1964. Nos. 4555, 4566, 4588, 5541 and 5572 have been preserved.

pp. 179–80

4700–4708

Churchward 2–8–0's, 5'8" driving wheels, express mixed traffic engines, fre-quently used on passenger trains. Built between 1919 and 1923, all were scrapped between 1962 and 1964.

p. 180

5600–5699, 6600–6699

Collett 0–6–2T's with $4'7\frac{1}{2}''$ wheels, built between 1924 and 1928. They were designed mainly for service in South Wales, although a few were to be found on other parts of the system. All withdrawn between 1962 and 1966. Nos. 5643 and 6697 have been preserved.

p. 181

5800–5819

Collett 0–4–2T's, built 1932–3, for branch line traffic. They were similar to the 1400 class, but were not motor fitted. With the exception of No. 5815, which lasted until 1961, all of the class were scrapped by the end of 1959.   **p. 181**

4900–4910, 4912–4999, 5900–5999, 6900–6999, 7900–7929

Collett 2-cylinder 4–6–0's, with 6'0" wheels, for general purpose express duties. The original engine, No. 4900 *Saint Martin*, was a reconstruction of a Churchward 'Saint' (see 2900 class, page 24). The remainder of the class was built between 1928 and 1950 and the engines were named after halls. The missing engine in the series, No. 4911, was destroyed in an air raid in 1941. Between 1946 and 1950 some of the class ran as oil burners and were renumbered temporarily in the 3900s, reverting to their original numbers on reconversion to coal burning. Those concerned were (with the temporary numbers in brackets): 4907 (3903), 4948 (3902), 4968 (3900), 4971 (3901), 4972 (3904), 5955 (3950), 5976 (3951), 5986 (3954), 6949 (3955), 6953 (3953), 6957 (3952). The prototype, No. 4900, together with No. 4940, were scrapped in 1959 and most of the others followed between then and 1965. Nos. 4930, 4983, 5900, 6960 and 6998 have been preserved.   **pp. 182–3**

5400–5424

Collett 0–6–0PT's for passenger work, motor fitted with 5'2" wheels. They were built between 1930 and 1935. The original engine, No. 5400, was a rebuild of 0–6–0PT No. 2062. Withdrawal of the class started in December 1956, but all scrapped 1962–4.   **p. 184**

6400–6439

Collett 0–6–0PT's for passenger work, motor fitted, with 4'7½" wheels. Built between 1932 and 1937. All withdrawn between 1958 and 1964. Nos. 6412, 6430 and 6435 have been preserved.   **p. 184**

7400–7449

Collett 0–6–0PT's for passenger work. They were similar to the 6400 class, having 4'7½" wheels, but not motor-fitted. Built 1936–50. All withdrawn between 1959 and 1965.   **p. 185**

3400–3409, 8400–8499, 9400–9499

0–6–0PT's, designed by Hawksworth, the last modification of a G.W.R. design dating back to the 1860s; several thousand, of different varieties, appeared all told. The first ten, Nos. 9400–9409, were built in 1947 and were superheated. A large order for 200 similar engines, but without superheaters, was then given to outside firms, the first being placed in service in 1949. Delivery was slow, however, and the final batch, Nos. 3400–3409, did not arrive until 1956, these being the last locomotives of pre-Nationalisation design to be constructed. Notwithstanding its comparatively recent construction, this class had a short life, due to dieselisation, and all the locomotives disappeared between 1959 and 1965. No. 9400 has been preserved. **p. 185**

6800–6879

Collett 2-cylinder 4–6–0's, with 5'8" wheels, for intermediate passenger duties. The class was built between 1936 and 1939 and named after granges. All withdrawn between 1960 and 1965. **p. 186**

7800–7829

2-cylinder 4–6–0's with 5'8" wheels, a slightly lighter version of the 'Granges', designed by Collett for use over main and cross-country lines restricted against the use of heavy engines, such as the former Cambrian and M. & S.W.J.R. systems. Nos. 7800–7819 were built in 1938–9 and Nos. 7820–7829 in 1950. The original intention was to construct 100 engines of each of the 'Grange' and 'Manor' classes to be numbered 6800–6899 and 7800–7899. They were intended to replace the 4300 class in passenger work. The order was suspended at the outbreak of war and, apart from constructing ten further 'Manors' in 1950, no more were built and the order was never completed. All withdrawn between 1963 and 1965. Nos. 7808, 7819 and 7827 have been preserved. **pp. 186–7**

9054, 9064/5, 9072/3/6, 9083/4/7/9, 9091

The survivors of Dean's 'Duke of Cornwall' class 4–4–0's, a series of 40 engines built between 1895 and 1899. They had outside frames and 5'8" driving wheels. Built for service over the steeply graded Cornwall lines, they were latterly used principally on the former Cambrian Railways. The majority of the class carried names associated with the West Country. Until 1946 they were numbered 3254, 3264, etc. All the surviving locomotives of this class were withdrawn by 1951. **p. 188**

9000–9028

Outside framed 4–4–0's with 5'8" wheels. Built nominally as new engines between 1936 and 1939, they were in fact reconstructions of the withdrawn 'Duke of Cornwall' class (see above) and 'Bulldogs' (see page 25), embodying the boilers of the former and frames of the latter. They were numbered 3200–3228 until 1946 and for a short time the first 12 were named after earls. These name plates, however, were very soon transferred to the newly built 'Castle' class engines 5043–5054, and they remained un-named. For a long time the class continued to be known as 'Earls', but more recently the name 'Dukedog' (a combination of 'Duke of Cornwall' and 'Bulldog') was widely applied. Nos. 9006/7 and 9019 were scrapped in 1948, the remainder followed between 1954 and 1960. No. 9017 has been preserved under its original number, 3217. **p. 189**

THE SOUTHERN GROUP

The Southern Group

At Nationalisation, the Southern Railway possessed 1,845 steam locomotives, of ninety main classes, many of which embraced several varieties of major and minor importance.

Upon amalgamation, the numbers of the S.R. engines ranged from 1 to 3744, together with Mr Bulleid's 'Pacific' and 'Austerity' 0-6-0 classes, which had been given separate series under a new system embodying a number prefix and a letter denoting the wheel arrangement, i.e. 21C represented 4-6-2, followed by the number of the engine in the series, such as 21C101. So far as the normal numerical series is concerned, the locomotives of each of the three main constituents of the Southern Railway were identifiable by their numbers, although new construction had filled in many of the blanks below 2000. Engines of the former London & South Western Railway had retained their original identification without alteration, with the exception of those on what was then the duplicate list consisting of old locomotives, previously known as 0298, etc., which were altered by the addition of 3000 to their existing numbers, becoming 3298, etc. All South Eastern & Chatham engines had been adjusted by having 1000 added to their old numbers, while similarly the London, Brighton & South Coast had been increased by 2000. Engines working in the Isle of Wight were placed in a special series numbered between W1 and W34. There were also a few departmental engines attached to the Service Department which had numbers with the suffix 'S' in the Service Vehicles List.

After the formation of British Railways, engines of the former Southern Railway were prefixed by the letter 'S' on being repainted, to distinguish them from engines of other groups bearing the same numbers. In April 1948, however, it was decided to bring all locomotives into one series by adopting the simple renumbering scheme which had previously been followed by the Southern and London & North Eastern Railways after the 1923 grouping. This involved the addition of an appropriate number of thousands to the old number, thus easily preserving the identity of the locomotive. In the case of the Southern Railway the alteration was by the addition of 30000 to the old number. Exceptions to this general rule were made for the above mentioned L.S.W.R. duplicate list and the new Bulleid engines. The former were completely renumbered into a new series ranging from 30564 to 30589, a block of numbers by this time blank in the L.S.W.R. list, while the Bulleid engines were given straightforward numbers from 33001, 34001, and 35001 onwards, in place of their former somewhat clumsy algebraic equations. Isle of Wight engines remained unaltered, retaining their 'W' section series. Two further additions to this stud, Nos. W35 and W36, were made in 1949.

It is interesting to observe that this principle of adding an additional figure in front of the original number had happened no less than three times to some of the old L.B.S.C.R. locomotives. To cite an example: amongst Mr Stroudley's well-known 'Terriers', *Fulham* started life in 1877 as No. 44. In 1902 it was transferred to the duplicate list of the time by becoming No. 644, the L.B.S.C.R. having adopted the system of transferring some of its older engines to the six hundreds. The Southern again renumbered it 2644 in 1937, and finally under British Railways it became No. 32644 in 1948.

Incidentally, No. 70, *Poplar*, of the same class, was sold to the Kent & East Sussex Railway in 1901, this little line remaining independent until Nationalisation in 1948. When the old engine returned to the fold it was placed in its rightful place in the list as No. 32670, having skipped the two intermediate renumberings when out of service with the L.B.S.C.R. and the Southern.

The only new engines of Southern Railway design to be constructed after the beginning of 1949 were some further 'Pacifics' of both 'West Country' and 'Merchant Navy' classes, and, of course, the 'Leader' 0–6–6–0T's, an ill-fated and somewhat unfortunate experiment, all of which had been on order before Nationalisation took effect. The last new Southern engine to be built was the 'Pacific' No. 34110, which appeared in 1950.

For the greater part of its twenty-five years' existence the Southern Railway had occupied itself mainly with electrification, with the result that new steam construction was kept to a minimum. The average age of the locomotives, in so far as passenger designs were concerned, was much older than that of the other three groups. The years both immediately preceding and following Nationalisation, had, however, seen the infusion of much new blood in the shape of large numbers of Bulleid 'Pacifics' and later of various new British Railways designs. Consequently, many of the well-tried old favourites went to the scrapheap, which, however regrettable from a sentimental point of view, was undoubtedly conducive to more efficient working.

From the late 1950s onwards a considerable number of new B.R. standard types appeared. Consequently the older pre-grouping types began to disappear more quickly and had almost all been eliminated by the end of 1965.

During this period all thirty unconventional 'Merchant Navies' and half the 110 'West Country' Bulleid Pacifics were rebuilt on more orthodox lines, and the streamlining removed. Many were very active on the main Bournemouth line right up to the end of steam working in July 1967. This route was the last fully steam-operated main line in the country, yet the old London & South Western had been almost the first railway to consider large-scale electrification.

Class List - Historical Data
List of Illustrations

30001–3, 30005, 30007–10, 30013, 30020, 30361/3/6/7

Adams' 5'7" 0–4–4T's, originally a class of 50 engines numbered 1–20, 61–80, 358–367, built between 1888 and 1896. 14 of the class surviving in 1948; all scrapped by 1951.

p. 193

30021–60, 30104–12, 30123–5/7–33, 30241–56, 30318–24, 30328, 30356/7, 30374–9, 30479–81, 30667–76

L.S.W.R. class M7, Drummond 0–4–4T's, built between 1896 and 1911, originally 105 in class. All still running in 1954 except 126, which was superheated in 1921 and scrapped in 1937, and 672, which fell down the lift shaft to the City Tube at Waterloo in 1948 and was cut up on the spot. The remainder went between 1957 and 1964, but No. 245 has been preserved in the U.K., No. 53 in the U.S.A.

pp. 194–5

30061–30074

U.S.A. 0–6–0T engines, a class of 14 locomotives acquired from the War Dept. in 1947 for shunting at Southampton Docks. Built by the Porter and Vulcan firms of the U.S.A. in 1942 and 1943. In 1963 they were superseded by diesels. Six–Nos. 30061/2/7, 30074, 30065 and 30070 were transferred to the Departmental list as DS233–38. The class was withdrawn 1962–7, but four have been preserved, Nos. 64, 72, DS237 and DS238.

p. 195

30081–30103, 30147, 30176

Adams and Drummond 0–4–0T's, built between 1891 and 1908 and classified B4 by the L.S.W.R. The Drummond engines were originally built with pop safety valves on the dome, but later the boilers of the survivors were interchanged. Fourteen locomotives were allocated to Southampton Docks and named, but when supplanted by the previous class and redrafted, the names were removed. All withdrawn 1948–63. Nos. 30096 and 30102 were sold out of service but later secured for preservation.

p. 196

30113–22, 30280–9, 30300–5, 30307, 30310–4, 30336–8, 30702–19, 30721–33

L.S.W.R. class T9, Drummond's 6'7" 4–4–0 express engine, built between 1899 and 1901. Superheated from 1924 onwards. Withdrawal of the class commenced in 1951 and was completed in 1961, but the last surviving engine was restored to L.S.W.R. livery as No. 120 and is preserved. **pp. 197–9**

30135, 30137, 30139–46, 30150–3, 30329, 30340/1/3/5, 30380, 30382–6, 30389–94

Drummond's 5'7" mixed traffic 4–4–0's L.S.W.R. Class K10, built between 1900 and 1902, of which there were originally 40 in the class. British Railways acquired 31 of them, but all were scrapped by 1951, and of these No. 30382 was the only one to receive its B.R. number. **p. 200**

30134, 30148, 30154–9, 30161, 30163–75, 30405–14, 30435–42

L.S.W.R. class L11, 5'7" mixed traffic 4–4–0's, built by Drummond between 1903 and 1907 as a class of 40 locomotives. They were a slightly enlarged version of the previous class. All these engines were scrapped between 1949 and 1952. **p. 201**

30177/9, 30181–3, 30192/3/7–9, 30200/3/4/7, 30212/3/6, 30221/3–5/9, 30230–3/6, W14–W36

Adams' 4'10" 0–4–4T's, class O2, originally a series of 60 engines numbered 177–236. By 1948, 48 were still in service. From 1923 onwards a number of locomotives of this class were gradually drafted to the Isle of Wight, renumbered in the special W series and given names. They were also fitted with enlarged bunkers. Nos. W35 (181) and W36 (198) were transferred in 1949 subsequent to Nationalisation. 30 of the class still remained in 1959, but by 1964 only 18 were still in service, all in the Isle of Wight. All withdrawn by 1967, when they were the oldest engines still in service on B.R. No. W24 has been preserved. **p.202–3**

30160, 30162, 30237–40, 30257–79, 30348 9, 30351 3 4

Adams' 0–6–0T's, L.S.W.R. class G6, built in 1894–1900. All came into B.R. stock, but all withdrawn by 1960. No. 272 latterly ran as Departmental No. DS3152. **p. 204**

30395–30404

Drummond's 6'0" 4–4–0, L.S.W.R. class S11, built 1903–4. The class was designed for service in the West of England, and was superheated in 1920–1. All of the class were scrapped in 1951 except one engine, No. 30400, which lasted until 1955. **p. 205**

30415–30434

Drummond's larger 6'7" 4–4–0's, class L12, built in 1904. They were given superheaters between 1915 and 1922. All were withdrawn from service in 1951, except No. 30415, scrapped in 1953, and No. 30434, which lasted until early 1955.

p. 206

30463–30472

Drummond's final design of 6'7" 4–4–0 locomotives, classified by the L.S.W.R. as D15. Built in 1912, they were an enlarged version of the previous class, and were his last engines. All the class were superheated in 1915–17. No. 463 was fitted for oil burning in 1946 and scrapped in 1951, without being reconverted or renumbered. The others all received their 30000 numbers, but all had gone by early 1956. All originally had 8-wheeled tenders, but in 1926 they were fitted with 6-wheelers.

p. 207

30306, 30308, 30309, 30315–17, 30325–7, 30339, 30346, 30350, 30352, 30355, 30368, 30687–701

L.S.W.R. 0–6–0 goods locomotive, designed by Drummond and built in 1897. Superheated between 1920 and 1927; No. 30688 was scrapped in 1957 after being involved in an accident and all the others had gone by 1963.

p. 208

30330–30334

L.S.W.R. class H15, Drummond's first 4–6–0's, built in 1905 as 4-cylinder engines, with 6'0" driving wheels. They were completely rebuilt in their present form with 2 cylinders in 1924–5. All withdrawn between 1956 and 1958, except No. 30331, which continued running until 1961.

p. 208

30335

Drummond's second class of 4–6–0 locomotive, a modified version of the 330 class. One engine only was built in 1907, designated class H15, with 4 cylinders and converted to a 2-cylinder machine in 1915. It had 6'0" driving wheels and was scrapped in 1959.

p. 209

30482–30491

Urie's first 4–6–0's, with 6'0" driving wheels and 2 cylinders, for mixed traffic duties. These engines were built new in this form, the two preceding Drummond classes being later altered to this design. All the engines became nominally one class (H15). No. 30491 had an N15 type boiler but was practically indistinguishable in appearance from her sisters. All taken out of traffic between 1955 and 1959 except Nos. 30489 and 30491 which lasted until 1961.

p. 209

30443–30447, 30459–30462

Originally ten engines with 6'7" wheels and 4 cylinders for express duties, these were Drummond's later 4–6–0's, built 1911–12. They were nicknamed 'Paddle-boxes' because of the heavy and cumbersome splashers with which they were first fitted. These were removed and the running plates raised in 1930 and 1931. Superheaters were added in 1915–18. No. 458 was destroyed in an air raid in 1940, and only Nos. 30446, 30447 and 30461 were actually renumbered. All were scrapped by 1951. Classified T14. **p. 210**

30448–30457

Southern Railway class N15, the original ten 'King Arthurs', built in 1925. The tenders were taken from ten 4-cylinder Drummond engines bearing the same numbers (448–457), which were broken up concurrently, or in some cases shortly after the appearance of the new engines. The class had 6'7" wheels and later had smokebox deflectors fitted. The withdrawal of the entire class was completed between 1958 and 1962. **p. 210**

30458

L.S.W.R. 0–4–0ST built in 1890 for the Southampton Dock Company. It was latterly numbered 3458 in the S.R. duplicate list, but with the B.R. renumbering of this group (see page 35) it received the number 30458. It was numbered outside the 30564 series because by coincidence this number happened to be blank, due to the war casualty mentioned in the T14 class. There was formerly a sister engine, No. 734, *Clausentum*, but this was scrapped in 1945. The pair were originally numbered 457 and 458 by the L.S.W.R. No. 30458 was scrapped in 1954. **p. 211**

30473–30478, 30521–30524

S.R. class H15, Maunsell modification of Urie 482 class, built in 1924. All were scrapped between 1959 and 1961. **p. 211**

30492–30495

Urie 4–8–0T engine, 5'1" wheels, 2 cylinders, built in 1921 for hump shunting in the then newly constructed Feltham marshalling yard. L.S.W.R. class G16. Nos. 30492/3 were scrapped in 1959 and the other pair in 1962. **p. 212**

30496–30515

Urie 5'7" express freight engine, L.S.W.R. class S15, built in 1920–1. Some of the class had the earlier Drummond 8-wheeled tenders as shown on page 209 and elsewhere. All withdrawn between 1961 and 1964. **p. 212**

30516–30520

L.S.W.R. class H16, Urie's 4–6–2T's, with 5'7" wheels built 1921 for short distance freight working from Feltham yard. All were withdrawn in 1962.

p. 213

30530–30549

0–6–0 freight locomotive, S.R. class Q, designed by Maunsell and built 1937–9. Withdrawn 1962–5. No. 30541 still in existence (1973) and may be preserved.

p. 213

30564–30581

Adams' 0–6–0 goods engines, built 1881–5, and known as the L.S.W.R. 0395 class. There were originally 70 engines in the class, of which 50 were sent to the Middle East during the First World War and never returned. Of the remainder, two were scrapped prior to 1948, leaving 18 which came into B.R. stock. The last of the class to remain in service was No. 30567, withdrawn in 1959. Formerly numbered in the L.S.W.R. duplicate list between 029 and 0515, they were later altered by the S.R. to 3029, etc., and finally renumbered by B.R. into one series as 30564–30581. The main variations in the class lay in the front overhang, which was considerably longer in the later engines, and in the types of boilers fitted. These, in most cases, had at various times been interchanged between different engines of the class.

pp. 214–5

30582–30584

Adams' 4–4–2T's, built 1882–5, originally 71 engines comprising L.S.W.R. class 0415. All were withdrawn, or sold, by the L.S.W.R. and S.R. by 1928, except Nos. 3125 and 3520, which were retained for working the Lyme Regis branch. A third engine was re-acquired by the S.R. in 1946. This had originally been sold to the Government in 1917 and resold in turn to the East Kent Railway. It was returned as No. 3488, having been originally L.S.W.R. No. 488. Although officially classified as 0415, this is not strictly correct as applied to the three surviving engines, as the original series were purely well-tank locomotives with smaller square rear splashers. The later examples had these splashers extended forward to provide small side tanks additional to the well-tanks for increased water supply. All three were withdrawn in 1961, No. 30583 being acquired by the privately owned Bluebell Railway as L.S.W.R. No. 488. **p. 216**

30585–30587

Beattie 2–4–0T's, a once numerous class used on suburban work in London and elsewhere, being designated by the L.S.W.R. as class 0298, the last 12 being built in 1874–5. All were scrapped as long ago as 1898, except three engines retained for working the Wenford Bridge mineral line in Cornwall on which they were engaged for 64 years. They were considerably rebuilt and renewed during the course of the years, having received Drummond boilers amongst other modifications. The three surviving engines were Nos. 0298, 0314 and 0329 (latterly 3298, etc.). All were finally withdrawn in 1962, but Nos. 30585 and 30587 have been preserved. **p. 217**

30588, 30589, 77S

L.S.W.R. class C14, Drummond 0–4–0T's, originally a class of ten engines, Nos. 736–745, built in 1906 as 2–2–0T's for rail motor work. Seven of the class were sold to the Government during the First World War and not returned. The remaining three, Nos. 741, 744 and 745, were converted to 0–4–0T's; Nos. 0741 and 0744, later Nos. 3741 and 3744, then Nos. 30588 and 30589, for shunting at Southampton, whilst the third was transferred to the Service Department in 1927 as 77S for use at Redbridge sleeper depot. All were scrapped between 1957 and 1959. **p. 218**

30618, 30627, 30629, 30636

Adams' 0–4–2 mixed traffic engines, originally known as 'Jubilees', classified by the L.S.W.R. as A12. There were originally 90 in the class, built between 1887 and 1895. In 1948 there were only four survivors and all these were withdrawn during that year without being renumbered. **p. 218**

30756

Former Plymouth, Devonport and South Western Junction Railway 0–6–0T, acquired by the L.S.W.R. in 1922 when it became No. 756. Built in 1907, scrapped in 1951. It was named *A. S. Harris*. **p. 219**

30757, 30758

Two 0–6–2T engines from the former P.D. & S.W.J.R., built in 1907 and named *Earl of Mount Edgcumbe* and *Lord St. Levan*. These locomotives became Nos. 757 and 758 in the L.S.W.R. and S.R. lists. They were scrapped in 1957. **p. 219**

30736–30755

Urie's express passenger 4–6–0's, with 6'7" wheels, built 1918–23. Originally L.S.W.R. class N15, they were later named by the S.R. and embodied in the 'King Arthur' class (see next class and also page 40). Later modifications included

42

a new design of chimney and smokebox wing-plates. Nos. 30740/5/8/9 and 30753 were running as oil burners in 1948, but were later reconverted to coal burners. All were taken out of service between 1953 and 1957. **p. 220**

30763–30792

Maunsell 'King Arthur', or N15, class (see Nos. 30448–30457, page 40) with modified cabs. Built in 1925 and fitted with bogie tenders. Although all the class was withdrawn between 1958 and 1962, No. 777 has been retained for preservation. **p. 221**

30793–30806

Similar to Nos. 30763–30792 but with 6-wheeled tenders. Built in 1926 for main line work on the Brighton section, but transferred elsewhere on electrification. All were taken out of service between 1959 and 1962. **p. 221**

30823–30847

Maunsell's 5'7" express freight engines. S.R. class S15, developed from Urie's 30496 series (see page 40). Built in 1927–36. Both of these classes were frequently used on passenger trains. Withdrawn 1962–5. No. 30841 has been preserved. **p. 222**

30850–30865

'Lord Nelson' class, Maunsell's 4-cylinder express 4–6–0's, built 1926–9. Later modifications included smokebox deflectors and double blast pipes with wide chimneys. No. 30859 had 6'3" driving wheels as against 6'7" for the rest of the class. No. 30860 had a slightly longer boiler. No. 30865 had the crank setting adjusted to give the normal four exhausts per revolution of the driving wheels, the others of the class giving eight blasts. All were withdrawn in 1961 and 1962, but No. 850 has been retained for preservation. **p. 222**

30900–30939

Maunsell 3-cylinder express 4–4–0's, 'Schools' class (S.R. class V), the last new design of this wheel arrangement to appear in this country. Built 1930–5, with 6'7" wheels. They performed much heavy express work on the S.E.C.R. section, particularly on the Hastings line, until replaced by diesel rail cars. The whole of the class was taken out of traffic in the years 1961–2. Three of the class have been preserved, Nos. 30925 and 30928 in this country and 30926 in the U.S.A. **p. 223**

Kent & East Sussex No. 4

Beattie 0–6–0ST, originally L.S.W.R. 335, built 1876. This locomotive was exchanged with the S.R. in 1932 for 0–8–0T No. 30949. Scrapped in 1948 without being allocated a B.R. number.   **p. 224**

30948

East Kent Railway No. 4, a 0–6–0T built in 1917. This line was merged with the S.R. on Nationalisation. The engine was scrapped in 1949 without receiving its new number.   **p. 224**

30949

0–8–0T *Hecate*, built in 1904 for the Kent and East Sussex Railway, but found too heavy for the line. Exchanged for the Beattie 0–6–0ST, K. & E.S.R. No. 4 with the S.R. in 1932, becoming S.R. No. 949. Scrapped in 1950 without receiving its new number.   **p. 225**

30950–30957

S.R. class Z, Maunsell 3-cylinder 0–8–0T, for heavy yard shunting, built in 1929. All were withdrawn in 1962.   **p. 225**

31002, 31028, 31031, 31042, 31078, 31105, 31151, 31215, 31231

S.E.C.R. Stirling 7′0″ 4–4–0's, originally class F (later class F1), built with domeless boilers and rounded cabs. A class of 88 engines built between 1883 and 1898 for the South Eastern Railway. All but 12 were rebuilt with domed boilers and new cabs by Wainwright and most of these later received extended smokeboxes. Eight engines survived to become B.R. stock, but the last was withdrawn in 1949, and only No. 31151 actually carried its B.R. number.   **p. 226**

31013, 31217, 31440/3/5/6/8–55/7/9

S.E.C.R. Stirling 7′0″ 4–4–0's built originally for the South Eastern Railway, an enlarged version of class F1 above. These were originally class B with domeless boilers, of which there were 29 engines built 1898–9. All but two were rebuilt with domed boilers by Wainwright and all of these later received extended smokeboxes. 16 engines survived to become B.R. stock, but the last was withdrawn in 1951.   **p. 226**

31003/7, 31014, 31039, 31041/4/6/8, 31051, 31064–6, 31080, 31093, 31106/8/9, 31123, 31238, 31248, 31258, 31316, 31369–74, 31377–81, 31384–6, 31388–91, 31395–8, 31425/6/8–30/2/4/7–9

Class O1, S.E.C.R. Stirling 0–6–0's, originally 122 in class, built with domeless boilers and rounded cabs 1878–99. Later survivors were all rebuilt with domed boilers and new cabs, and 55 came into B.R. stock in 1948. Three of these had been sold to the East Kent Railway and were returned to B.R. stock with their original numbers plus 30000, but only one, No. 31383, was renumbered. Many of the others were scrapped with their old S.R. numbers. All withdrawn by 1961, but No. 31065 has been preserved as S.E.C.R. 65. **p. 227**

31004, 31018, 31033/7/8, 31054/9, 31061/3/8, 31071, 31086, 31090, 31102, 31112/3, 31150, 31191, 31218/9, 31221/3/5/7/9, 31234, 31242–5, 31252/3/5–7, 31260/7/8, 31270–2/7, 31280/7, 31291/3/4/7/8, 31317, 31460/1, 31480/1/6, 31495/8, 31508, 31510/3, 31572/3/5/6, 31578–85, 31588–90/2/3, 31681–4, 31686–95, 31711–25

Wainwright class C 0–6–0 general purpose engine used on all kinds of duties. 109 engines of the class were built 1900–8; two were scrapped prior to 1948, while one was converted to a saddle tank (see No. 31685, page 48). In 1964 only Nos. 31271 and 31592 remained, as Departmental engines DS240 and DS239. The latter has been preserved and restored as S.E.C.R. 592. **p. 228**

31027, 31178, 31323/5, 31555–8

Class P light 0–6–0T's with 3'9" wheels designed by Wainwright. Eight engines were built from 1909 to 1910 for rail motor working on branch lines, latterly used for light shunting. All of the class were scrapped, or sold out of service, by 1961. Nos. 27, 178, 323 and 556 have been preserved. **p. 228**

31005, 31016, 31158, 31161/2/4, 31177, 31182/4, 31193, 31239, 31259, 31261/3/5/6/9, 31295, 31305–11, 31319–22, 31324/6–9, 31500/3, 31512/7–23, 31530–3, 31540–4/6/8, 31550–4

0–4–4T's, class H, designed by Wainwright, consisting of 66 locomotives built 1904–15. 64 came into B.R. stock in 1948. Most ran until the early 1960s. The last survivor, 31263, withdrawn in 1964, has been preserved and restored as S.E.C.R. 263. **p. 229**

31010, 31047, 31069, 31107, 31127/8, 31147, 31154, 31174, 31335/7/9, 31340

Stirling 0–6–0T's, class R1, originally class R with domeless boilers, a class of 25 engines built 1888–98. The 13 survivors (12 were still running in 1955) which

45

came into B.R. stock had all been rebuilt with domed boilers, but of those scrapped many had never been rebuilt. The last survivors went in 1960.

pp. 230–1

31302

0–4–0T crane engine, built in 1881 and scrapped in 1949. A similar engine, No. 409, built 1896, was scrapped in 1935. **p. 231**

31057, 31075, 31092, 31477, 31488, 31490/3/6, 31501, 31549, 31574/7, 31586, 31591, 31728–34, 31737/8, 31740/4/6/8, 31750

Wainwright 4–4–0's, class D, built 1901–7. Originally there were 51 engines in the class, of which 21 were rebuilt as class D1 1921–7 (see below). All of the unrebuilt engines, except No. 1742, came into B.R. stock. All withdrawn by 1957. No. 31737 has been preserved and restored as S.E.C.R. 737. **p. 232**

31145, 31246/7, 31470, 31487/9, 31492/4, 31502/5/9, 31545, 31727, 31735/6/9, 31741/3/5/9

D class engines, rebuilt as class D1 between 1921 and 1927, with superheaters, piston valves and other modifications. One engine, No. 1747, was scrapped prior to 1948, but all the rest of the rebuilt engines came into B.R. stock. All were scrapped by 1961. **p. 232**

31036, 31157/9, 31166, 31175/6, 31273/5, 31315, 31491, 31514–6, 31547, 31587

Wainwright 4–4–0's, class E, built 1905–9. There were originally 26 engines in the class, of which 11 were rebuilt 1919–21 as class E1 (see below). The last surviving unrebuilt locomotive of this class, No. 31166, was scrapped in 1955.

p. 233

31019, 31067, 31160/3/5, 31179, 31497, 31504/6/7, 31511

E class engines rebuilt 1919–21 with superheaters, piston valves and other modifications and designated as class E1. All the class was withdrawn by 1961.

p. 233

31595–31599

Class J 0–6–4T's, designed by Wainwright and built in 1913. All scrapped in 1950 and 1951. **p. 234**

31602, 31604, 500S (originally **607**)

L.C.D.R. Kirtley 0–6–0T's class T, originally ten engines built 1879–93. The three surviving locomotives taken over by B.R. were all scrapped during 1950–1.

p. 234

31658–31663, 31665–7, 31670–5

Kirtley L.C.D.R. 0–4–4T's, class R, built 1891. There were originally 18 engines in this class, all of which were scrapped by 1956.

p. 235

31696–31700, 31703–10

Kirtley design of 0–4–4T, built in 1900, after the formation of the S.E.C.R. class R1, originally 15 engines. All were scrapped by 1956.

p. 235

31790–31809

Class U, built as 2–6–4T's, No. 790 by the S.E.C.R. in 1917, the others by the S.R. in 1925–6. All were converted to 2–6–0 tender engines after No. 800's derailment at high speed in 1927. As tank engines they were named after rivers. Withdrawn 1963–6.

p. 236

31610–31639

Maunsell 2-cylinder 2–6–0's class U, with 6′0″ wheels. Built 1928–31 to the design of the converted engines mentioned above, with a few minor modifications. All withdrawn 1963–6. No. 31618 has been preserved.

p. 236

31890

Class U1 engine, with 6′0″ wheels and 3-cylinders, built originally as a 2–6–4T. Converted to a tender engine in 1928 after the accident to the similar U class engine. Withdrawn 1963.

p. 237

31891–31910

Class U1, built 1931–2, with slight modifications, to the design of the prototype conversion, No. 31890. All were withdrawn in 1962–3.

p. 237

31810–21, 31823–75

Maunsell class N 2–6–0 mixed traffic locomotive with 5′6″ wheels, built 1917–23. The last 50 of the class were constructed at Woolwich Arsenal and not acquired by the S.R. until 1925. All withdrawn 1963–6. No. 31874 still in existence in 1973, with possibility of preservation.

p. 238

31400–31414

Class N, additional engines, built 1932–4, with a modified design of the tenders. All withdrawn 1962–6. **p. 239**

31822, 31876–31880

3-cylinder 2–6–0's, with 5′6″ wheels, class N1. The original engine of this class was built by the S.E.C.R. in 1922, the last five by the S.R. in 1930. All were withdrawn in 1962. **p. 239**

31685

Class S 0–6–0ST, rebuilt 1917 from Wainwright class C 0–6–0, the only engine so reconstructed. Scrapped 1951. **p. 240**

31911–31925

Maunsell 3-cylinder 2–6–4T's, class W, built 1931–2. The class incorporated side tanks and other parts of some of the converted 'River' class 2–6–4T's (see page 47), but in view of the unfortunate history of that class the new engines were confined entirely to freight work. All withdrawn during 1963–4. **p. 240**

31760–31781

Class L, Wainwright's last 4–4–0's for the S.E.C.R., built 1914. The whole class was scrapped between 1956 and 1961. **p. 241**

31753–9, 31782–9

Class L1, Maunsell design 4–4–0's, built 1926. All were scrapped between 1959 and 1961. **p. 241**

32001–32010

L.B.S.C.R. Marsh design 4–4–2T's, class I1X, with 5′6″ wheels, built in 1907 and reboilered 1929–31. All of the class were scrapped between 1948 and 1951. **p. 242**

32021–3, 32025–30, 32075–91

Class I3 L.B.S.C.R. Marsh express 4–4–2T's with 6′7½″ wheels built 1907–13. Although No. 2024 had been scrapped in 1944, most of the remaining 26 engines survived to be renumbered into B.R. stock, but all were withdrawn by 1952. **p. 243**

32037–32039

Marsh 'Atlantics', originally a class of five engines, Nos. 37–41, built 1905–6 and designated class H1. Nos. 2040 and 2041 were withdrawn in 1944 and the three survivors in 1951. The last three were numbered into B.R. stock. **p. 244**

32100–32109

Billinton 0–6–0T's, class E2, built 1913–16. Scrapped between 1961 and 1963.
p. 245

32044, 32051, 32054, 32062, 32063, 32068, 32074

Survivors of a class of 33 locomotives built between 1899 and 1902 as L.B.S.C.R. Nos. 42–74 and classified B4 by the parent company. Of the remainder, 12 had been rebuilt as class B4X and the others scrapped before 1948. The last of the unrebuilt engines went in 1951, none of them having received its allocated B.R. number. **p. 246**

32043, 32045, 32050, 32052, 32055–6, 32060, 32067, 32070–3

Class B4X, rebuilds of class B4 above, reconstructed between 1922 and 1924. The last of the class disappeared in 1951. **p. 247**

32421–32426

Later Marsh 'Atlantics', class H2, built 1911–12. No. 2423 was scrapped in 1949 without receiving its B.R. number. Four more went in 1956, but No. 32424 survived until 1958, the last 'Atlantic' engine to run in ordinary service in Great Britain **p. 247**

32097, 32112/3, 32122, 32127–9, 32133/8/9, 32141/2/5/7, 32151/3/6, 32606/9. 32689–91/4, W1–W4

Class E1, Stroudley 0–6–0T's, a class of 73 engines built 1874–84. Four of the class still remaining in 1960, and one of them, No. 32694, lasted until 1961.
p. 248

32160, 32162, 32164

Stroudley designed 0–6–0T's similar to the above class, but not built until 1891 and slightly modified in various details by Billinton. Originally six engines, Nos. 159–164 (they were also classified E1), the three survivors were all scrapped by 1951. **p. 249**

32094–6, 32124, 32135, 32608, 32610, 32695–7

Class E1R, rebuilds of class E1 (see page 49), reconstructed 1927–8 with additional trailing wheels for service in the West Country. All taken out of service between 1955 and 1959. **p. 249**

32215, 32234/5/9, 32252/3/9, 32269, 32274, 32283/6/9, 32299, 32358/9, 32361, 32605, 32699, 700S, 701S

Class D1, comprising the survivors of Stroudley's 0–4–2T's built 1873–87. Scrapping began as long ago as 1903, but the majority of the class were withdrawn by the S.R. between 1923 and 1947. None of the remainder received their B.R. allocated numbers and all were scrapped by 1950. **pp. 250–1**

32300–3, 32306–9

Marsh 0–6–0's, class C3, originally a class of ten engines, Nos. 300–9, built in 1906. The last of the class was scrapped in 1952. **p. 252**

32435, 32436, 32533

Three engines of Billinton's 0–6–0's, class C2, remaining in unrebuilt form. The class originally comprised 55 locomotives, built 1893–1902 by the Vulcan Foundry and always known as the 'Vulcans'. The greater part were rebuilt with large boilers between 1908–40 (see class C2X below), while these three unrebuilt engines were all scrapped by 1950. **p. 252**

32434/7/8, 32440–51, 32521–9, 32532, 32534–41, 32543–54

Class C2X, rebuilt 'Vulcans' of class C2 (see above), comprising 45 engines. All were withdrawn between 1957 and 1962. **p. 253**

32325

Marsh 4–6–2T, class J1, built 1910 and scrapped in 1951. **p. 254**

32326

Class J2, similar to No. 32325, built in 1912 with Walschaert's valve gear, and scrapped in 1951. **p. 254**

32327–32333

Class N15X, originally built between 1914 and 1922 as 4–6–4T engines, they were converted in 1935–6 to 4–6–0 tender locomotives consequent to the electrification of the Brighton and Eastbourne main lines, on which they were hitherto employed. All were scrapped between 1955 and 1957. **p. 255**

32337–32353

Billinton 2–6–0's, class K, built 1913–21. The whole class was withdrawn *en bloc* in December 1962. **p. 255**

32364–8, 32370–4, 32376–80, 32383–91, 32393–5, 32398

Class D3, Billinton 0–4–4T's, originally a class of 36 engines, Nos. 363–398, built 1892–6. All of the survivors were scrapped by B.R. by 1955. **p. 256**

32397

Originally class D3 rebuilt with large boiler in 1909 and designated class D3X. Scrapped 1948 as 2397. No. 2396 was also similarly rebuilt at the same time, but this one was withdrawn in 1937. **p. 256**

32408–10, 32412–18

Class E6, Billinton 0–6–2T's with 4'6" wheels, for freight work, built in 1904–5. The class was scrapped between 1958 and 1962. **p. 257**

32407, 32411

Two engines rebuilt in 1911 from class E6 above and classified E6X. No. 32407 was scrapped in 1957 and No. 32411 in 1959. **p. 257**

32463–5, 32467–76, 32479–82, 32484–8, 32490–32520, 32556–32566, 32577–82

Billinton 0–6–2T passenger engines with 5'0" driving wheels, built 1897–1903. Four of this class E4 were rebuilt as class E4X (see page 52); the engine bearing the missing number, No. 2483, was scrapped in 1944, otherwise the whole of the class was still running in 1954, but only about 30 remained in 1961. The last of these went in 1963. No. 473 has been preserved by the Bluebell Railway, with its old name *Birch Grove* restored. **pp. 258–9**

32466, 32477, 32478, 32489

Class E4X, four engines of class E4 rebuilt 1909–12. All of these withdrawn 1955–9. **p. 259**

51

32165–70, 32453–62

Billinton 0-6-2T's, similar to class E4 (see page 51), but with 4′6″ driving wheels for freight work. Class E3, built 1894–5. No. 2457 was scrapped in 1949, and the rest went between 1955 and 1959. **p. 260**

32399, 32400, 32402, 32404–6, 32567/8, 32571–5, 32583–5, 32587–94

Billinton 0–6-2T's, class E5, with 5′6″ wheels. Originally a class of 30 engines built 1902–4 for fast passenger work. All scrapped by 1956. **p. 260**

32401, 32570, 32576, 32586

Four engines rebuilt in 1911 from class E5 and re-classified E5X. All withdrawn 1954–6. **p. 261**

32595–6, 32598–9, 32601–4

Marsh 4-4-2T's for the L.B.S.C.R., similar to Nos. 32001–32010, but with longer wheelbase. There were originally ten engines numbered 595–604, built 1906–7 and reboilered 1925–8. The survivors of the class were scrapped between 1948 and 1951. **p. 242**

32635, 32636, 32640/4/6/7, 32650/5, 32661/2, 32670/7/8, DS681

Class A1X, Stroudley 'Terriers', originally 50 engines numbered 35–84, built 1872–80. Some were scrapped or sold as long ago as 1899. 12 of the class still in service in 1955. No. 32650 was DS515 in the service list until 1953, at which time No. 32659 became DS681. No. 32635 was DS377 until 1959. Nos. 32646 and 32677 were W8 and W13 in the Isle of Wight list until 1949, when they were returned to the mainland and reverted to their places in the L.B.S.C.R. series. Nos. 32636, 32646, 32650, 32662, 32670 and 32678 were still running in the summer of 1963, the oldest British Railways engines in service and the only L.B.S.C.R. locomotives still extant. These were all withdrawn, however, in November 1963 on the cessation of service on the Hayling Island Branch, which was their last regular duty. No less than ten have been preserved, as static exhibits or working locomotives. These are Nos. 40, 46, 50, 55, 62, 70, 72, 78 and also 54 and 82 (see below). Some have been restored to L.B.S.C. yellow livery, with former names. **pp. 262–3**

DS680, LBSC 82

'Terriers' retaining short smokebox and classified A1. DS680 was withdrawn in 1963 and repainted in its original colours as No. 54 *Waddon* for preservation in

Canada. No. 82 *Boxhill* (preserved by B.R.) is mentioned for completeness, but it was withdrawn in 1946, never coming into B.R. stock. **p. 263**

34001–34110

Bulleid light 'West Country Pacifics' built between 1945 and 1950. The first 70 were turned out by the S.R. as Nos. 21C101–21C170. Nos. 34049–34090 and 34109/10 are usually referred to as the 'Battle of Britain' class, owing to the association of their names, but apart from this they are identical with the 'West Countries', which are named after West Country holiday resorts. In common with the Merchant Navies (see below), of which they were a lighter version, these engines had many unusual features, such as chain-driven valve gear, totally enclosed in an oil bath, and streamlining. Fifty-five were completely rebuilt 1957–61 on more orthodox lines. The whole class was taken out of service 1963–7. No. 34064 latterly ran with a Giesl ejector. Nos. 34051 and 34092 (not rebuilt) and 34016 and 34039 (rebuilt) have been preserved; others may also be preserved.

pp. 264–5

35001–35030

Bulleid's heavy 'Pacifics', 'Merchant Navy' class, built between 1941 and 1948. The first 20 of the class were turned out by the S.R. as 21C1 to 21C20. Early in 1956 No. 35018 was modified in the same way as the 'West Countries' (see above); by the end of 1959 so was the whole class. All withdrawn 1964–7. Nos. 35005 and 35028 have been preserved; others still extant in Barry scrapyard in 1973 may also be preserved. **pp. 265–6**

33001–33040

Class Q1, Bulleid's 'Austerity' 0–6–0's built in 1942 as C1–C40. Withdrawn 1963–6. No. 33001 has been preserved. **p. 267**

36001–36003

'Leader' class, Bulleid's experimental 0–6–6–0T engines built in 1949. Five engines were ordered, but only three were completed and the last two were never steamed. All were scrapped in 1951. **p. 267**

THE L.M.S. GROUP

The L.M.S. Group

At Nationalisation, the London, Midland & Scottish Railway had some 7,850 locomotives of over 100 main classes, many of which embraced several variations of major and minor importance.

The L.M.S. numbering scheme ranged from 1 to 28622. For a short time these numbers were retained, with the addition of the prefix 'M' to denote L.M.S. origin and to distinguish them from locomotives of the other three groups bearing the same numbers. In March 1948, a general renumbering scheme was devised which, so far as the L.M.S. group was concerned, involved in most cases the simple addition of 40000 to the old numbers. As only the block 40000 to 59999 was allocated to the L.M.S., complete renumbering of engines in the 20000s into a new series in the 58000s was involved. All of these were old classes and comprised principally the surviving engines of a number of Midland and L.N.W.R. designs, mostly 0-6-0 tender engines, together with a few old passenger engines and a collection of miscellaneous tanks. At the same time other classes were renumbered in this series to make way for further new engines under construction, or on order. These included Midland 0-4-4T's, ranging from 1239 to 1430, which were renumbered from 58030 onwards to provide room for further Ivatt 2-6-2T's in the 41200 series. Also the Midland Johnson class 2 Goods, numbered between 22900 and 23018, and 3021 upwards (the earlier ones had already been altered by the addition of 20000) were for convenience all given a new series, 58114–58310.

Another renumbering, altering the L.T.S.R. 4-4-2T's from 2092–2160 to 41910–41978, made way for further 2 6 4T's in the 42000s and 42100s. L.M.S. diesel shunters hitherto numbered in the 7000s were put into a completely new British Railways' series in the 10000s, allocated under the new scheme to diesel, diesel-electric and gas-turbine engines.

Construction of L.M.S. classes proceeded steadily for the first four years of Nationalisation until supplanted by the new British Railways' designs which began to appear in 1951. However, as late as between October 1953 and January 1954 five new 0-4-0ST's based on a 1932 design were completed at Horwich, and the final one, No. 47009, was the last new engine to be given a number in the 40000 series, all new standard designs being numbered from 70000 upwards. These five engines differed in some respects from their predecessors and may be said to constitute a new variety of L.M.S. design which did not appear until six years after the L.M.S. had ceased to exist.

The early years of Nationalisation saw a great thinning out of the older designs, particularly those dating back before 1923 to the pre-grouping era, and the introduction of B.R. standard types inevitably resulted in the wholesale scrapping of some post-grouping classes. Of all four groups, however, engines of L.M.S. origin and design outlived most of their rivals, and indeed by the end of 1967 were practically the only ones remaining. These consisted largely of the well-tried and ubiquitous class 5 4–6–0's and class 8 2–8–0's, which not only took their place alongside standard B.R. types, but actually very considerably exceeded them in numbers at the end of steam working in August 1968.

Class List - Historical Data
List of Illustrations

40001–40070

Fowler 2–6–2T built by L.M.S. between 1930 and 1932. Withdrawals commenced in 1959, during which year nearly half the class were withdrawn; the others followed between 1960 and 1962. **pp. 271–2**

40071–40144

Stanier 2–6–2T with domeless boiler built by L.M.S. in 1935. All were withdrawn between 1959 and 1962. **pp. 272–3**

40145–40209

Stanier 2–6–2T built by L.M.S. in 1937 and 1938. Similar to 40071 class, but with domed boiler. The whole class was withdrawn between 1959 and 1962. **pp. 272–3**

40322–40326, and between 40332 & 40562

Midland class 2 superheated 4–4–0. Deeley rebuilds of Johnson engines, originally built between 1882 and 1901, but rebuilt from 1912 onwards. Nos. 40322–40326 were S.D.J.R. engines until 1930, but were similar to the M.R. locomotives of this class. There were 165 engines in 1948, but many were later scrapped, leaving only about six in stock in 1961 and by 1963 these had also gone. **p. 274**

40383, 40385, 40391

Three surviving Midland unsuperheated 4–4–0's. Built in 1888, they were rebuilt 1909–11. Nos 385 and 391 were scrapped in 1949 without being renumbered, and No. 40383 in 1952. **p. 273**

40563–40700

L.M.S. development of Midland class 2 4–4–0, built between 1928 and 1932. Nos. 40633–40635 were originally S.D.J.R. engines. Nos. 591 and 639 were scrapped in 1934 after being involved in an accident at Glasgow, and No. 40662 was withdrawn in September 1954. General withdrawal of the class commenced in 1959 and was completed in 1962.   **p. 275**

Between 40711 & 40762

22 survivors of an original total of 80 engines. Johnson's class 3 Belpaire 4–4–0's, built for the M.R. between 1900 and 1905, 73 of them receiving superheaters between 1911 and 1924. All since scrapped, No. 40726, the last survivor, being withdrawn in August 1952.   **p. 276**

41000–41044

Johnson and Deeley 3-cylinder compound locomotives, built by the Midland 1901–9. All withdrawn between 1948 and 1953, but the original engine has been retained and in 1959 was restored to its original condition as M.R. No. 1000 and used for working enthusiasts' specials. It has now been preserved.   **p. 277**

40900–40939, 41045–41199

L.M.S. development of M.R. compound, built between 1924 and 1932. Scrapping commenced in 1952 and, by the beginning of 1960, less than half a dozen still remained in service, the last survivor going in 1961.   **p. 278**

41200–41329

Ivatt 2–6–2T, for branch line work, built by L.M.S. in 1946. Construction was continued by B.R. until 1952, when it was superseded by the almost exactly similar new standard 84000 class. Nos. 41210–41229 and 41270–41289 were motor-fitted for pull-and-push working. All withdrawn 1962–7. Nos. 41241, 41298 and 41312 have been preserved.   **p. 279**

41509, 41516, 41518, 41523

Four remaining survivors of a class of 28 small 0–4–0ST's for shunting in docks and brewery yards, etc., built by the M.R. between 1883 and 1903. No. 1509 was scrapped in 1949, and Nos. 41518 and 41523 early in 1955. No. 41516 survived until 1958. Nearly all the remainder of the class had disappeared before 1930.   **p. 280**

41528–41537

Midland 0–4–0T's, built between 1907 and 1922 for shunting in brewery yards, docks, and other places where sharp curves are found. All scrapped 1957–66.   **p. 279**

Between 41660 & 41895

95 survivors of 240 engines built by S. W. Johnson for the M.R. between 1878 and 1899. Seven of these engines, Nos. 41708, 41712, 41734, 41763, 41804, 41835 and 41844, were still in service early in 1964, of which No. 41708, built in 1880, held the distinction of being the oldest running on B.R. They were not officially withdrawn until the end of 1966. No. 41708 has been preserved.

pp. 281–2

41900–41909

Ten 0–4–4T's built by Sir W. A. Stanier for the L.M.S. in 1932. Nos. 41901–41909 were withdrawn *en bloc* in December 1959, leaving only No. 41900 in service, which lasted until 1962.   **p. 283**

41910–41926

17 engines surviving of a total of 18 L.T. & S.R. 'Intermediate' class, built 1900–3, late L.M.S. numbers 2092–2104, 2106–2109. Only Nos. 41922, 41923 and 41925 actually carried their new numbers and all the class was scrapped by 1953.   **p. 283**

41953–41968

Large L.T. & S.R. 4–4–2T's. Nos. 41953–41964 were rebuilt from smaller class (originally constructed 1897–8), but Nos. 41965–41968 were built new in 1909. Late L.M.S. numbers 2135–2150. All scrapped by 1954 except No. 41966, which has since been restored as L.T. & S.R. No. 80 *Thundersley* for preservation.

p. 284

41928–41952, 41969–41978

Large L.T. & S.R. 4–4–2T type perpetuated by the L.M.S., with additional engines constructed 1923–30. Late L.M.S. numbers 2110–2134, 2151–2160. All were scrapped by 1960.   **p. 284**

41980–41993

14 0–6–2T's built by the L.T. & S.R. and M.R. between 1903 and 1912. Former L.M.S. numbers 2180–2193; all withdrawn in 1958–9, except No. 41981, which lasted until 1962.   **p. 285**

42050–42299, 42673–42699

Fairburn 2–6–4T's built by the L.M.S. and B.R. between 1945 and 1951. All withdrawn between 1961 and 1967. Nos. 42073 and 42085 have been preserved.

p. 285

42300–42424

Fowler parallel boiler 2–6–4T's built by the L.M.S. between 1927 and 1934. All scrapped between 1959 and 1966. **p. 286**

42425–42494, 42537–42672

Stanier 2-cylinder 2–6–4T's built 1935–43. Nos. 42537–42544 originally had domeless boilers of the type shown in the lower illustration on page 287, but one or two of this batch later had domes in conformity with the rest of the class. Withdrawn 1961–7. **p. 287**

42500–42536

Stanier 3-cylinder 2–6–4T's built in 1934 for the Tilbury section. All originally had domeless boilers, but a few later carried domes. The whole of the class was taken out of service in 1961 and 1962 upon electrification of the L.T. & S.R. section. No. 42500 has been preserved. **p. 287**

42700–42944

Horwich design 2–6–0 engines built by the L.M.S. between 1926 and 1932. Withdrawn 1962–7. No. 42700 has been preserved. **p. 288**

42945–42984

Stanier 2–6–0 locomotives built 1933–4. Withdrawn 1963–7. No. 42968 has been preserved. **p. 289**

43000–43161

Ivatt class 4 2–6–0's. First three engines turned out by the L.M.S. in December 1947, the remainder built under B.R. auspices from 1948 to 1952. Withdrawn 1963–8. No. 43106 has been preserved. **pp. 289–90**

43137 & between **43174** & **43189**

11 engines, Johnson 4′11″ 0–6–0's, built for the M.R. between 1885 and 1888 and later rebuilt with larger class 3 boilers. No. 43137 later became No. 43750,

consequent on construction of new 2–6–0 class above. Seven engines were still in service at the beginning of 1960, but all had gone by 1962. **p. 291**

Between **43191** & **43833**

387 surviving engines, similar to preceding class, but with 5'3" wheels. Those numbered up to 43763 were rebuilds of Johnson's smaller class 2 engines (see present series commencing at 58114) built originally in 1888–1902, but from 43765 onwards (built 1903–8) they were built new as class 3. Over 200 were still active early in 1960. By 1963 these had dwindled to less than a dozen, of which three only, Nos. 43620, 43637 and 43669, remained early in 1964, the last examples of the once numerous Johnson goods totalling 935 engines. They were withdrawn later that year. **p. 291**

43835–44026

192 engines built by the Midland to Sir Henry Fowler's design between 1911 and 1922. All still in service until May 1954, when the first of the class to be withdrawn was taken out of service. Over 70 had been scrapped by the beginning of 1960, withdrawal being completed by 1965. No. 43924 has been preserved. **p. 292**

44027–44606

M.R. design perpetuated by the L.M.S. and constructed between 1924 and 1940, except for Nos. 44557–44561 which were built for the S.D.J.R. in 1922. The final total of 772 engines was at that time the highest of any class in the country. Withdrawal began in 1959 and was completed in 1966. No. 44027 has been preserved. **p. 292**

44658–45499

842 engines constructed by the L.M.S. and B.R. between 1934 and 1951. There are a number of sub-divisions in this class provided by differences in the boiler mountings, special valve gears, roller bearings, double chimneys and various combinations of these features. Withdrawal began in 1962, but 150 were still at work in early 1968, when they too were all withdrawn. Twelve have been preserved, several in working condition, some restored to L.M.S. livery. These are Nos. 44767, 44806, 44871, 44932, 5000, 5025, 45110, 45212, 5231, 45305, 45407 and 5428. **pp. 293–5**

45500–45551

Fowler 3-cylinder 4–6–0 locomotives 'Baby Scot' or 'Patriot' class, built between 1930 and 1933. The whole of the class was taken out of traffic between 1960 and 1962. **pp. 296–7**

45552–45742

Stanier 'Jubilee' class, built 1934–6. Withdrawal 1961–7. Nos. 5690, 5593 and 5596 have been preserved in L.M.S. maroon livery and in working order.

pp. 297–8

46004

The sole survivor of the L.N.W.R. 'Claughton' class, originally totalling 130 engines; they were built between 1913 and 1922, many being rebuilt later with larger boilers. Scrapped in 1949, as 6004. **p. 299**

46100–46169

Fowler's 'Royal Scot' design for the L.M.S., built 1927–30, later rebuilt with taper boiler. Withdrawn 1962–5. Nos. 6100 and 6115 have been preserved, restored to L.M.S. maroon livery. **pp. 299–300**

46170

Originally constructed in 1929 as a high pressure engine, No. 6399 '*Fury*', and rebuilt in its present form in 1935. Withdrawn in 1962. **p. 300**

46200, 46201, 46203–46212

The original series of L.M.S. 'Pacifics', 'Princess' class, constructed by Sir W. A. Stanier in 1933 and 1935. All were withdrawn in 1961–2. Nos. 6201 and 6203 have been preserved, restored to L.M.S. maroon livery. **p. 301**

46202

Built in 1935 as a turbine-driven engine and ran in this form, with slight modifications, until 1952. The locomotive was rebuilt in that year to ordinary reciprocating propulsion, but broken up after being severely damaged in the Harrow accident in October 1952. **p. 302**

46220–46229, 46235–46248

Enlarged Stanier 'Pacifics', 'Coronation' class, built between 1938 and 1943. The original streamlined casings were removed between 1946 and 1949. Withdrawn 1962–4. Nos. 46229 and 46235 have been preserved. **p. 303**

46230–46234, 46249–46255

'Duchess' class 'Pacifics', built 1938–46, very similar to the 'Coronation' class, but never streamlined. Withdrawn 1962–4. **p. 304**

46256, 46257

The last two L.M.S. 'Pacifics', constructed in 1947 and 1948, and distinguished from their predecessors by the altered rear end and cab, etc. Both engines were withdrawn during 1964.   **p. 304**

46400–46527

Ivatt's light class 2 2–6–0, built by L.M.S. and B.R. 1946–52. Superseded by the very similar standard 78000 class. Withdrawn 1963–7. Nos. 6441 (restored in L.M.S. maroon), 46443, 46447, 46464, 46512 and 46521 have been preserved.   **pp. 305–6**

Between 46601 & 46757

43 surviving engines of a class of 160 L.N.W.R. 2–4–2T's built between 1890 and 1897. All of the class had been scrapped by 1955.   **p. 306**

46762

The only surviving engine of a small stock of locomotives acquired by the L.M.S from the Wirral Railway in 1923. It was originally a L. & Y.R. engine, sold to the Wirral before amalgamation and actually formed part of the class commencing at 50621 (see page 68). The reason for the odd number is that all Wirral engines were renumbered by the L.M.S. in the L.N.W.R. series, but the engine also had a number actually allocated to it in its rightful series, viz. 10638, which it never carried. Withdrawn in 1952.   **p. 307**

Between 46876 & 46931

Fifteen survivors of a L.N.W.R. class of 5'0" 0–6–2T's, of which 80 were built between 1898 and 1902. All scrapped by 1953.   **p. 307**

47000–47004

Built by Kitson's for the L.M.S. in 1932. 0–4–0ST's for dock shunting, colliery lines, etc., with severe curvature. Withdrawn 1964–6.   **p. 308**

47005–47009

Five similar engines, but with larger tanks and other detail alternations, built at Horwich between October 1953 and January 1954. The last new engines of basically L.M.S. design to be built. All withdrawn 1963–6.   **p. 308**

65

47160–47169

Fowler 0–6–0T's with short wheelbases for dock working, built in 1928. Scrapping commenced in 1959; all had gone by 1964.   **p. 309**

47180–47183

Sentinel two-speed shunters built for the L.M.S. in 1930. All of the class were withdrawn between 1953 and 1956.   **p. 309**

47184

Sentinel single-speed shunter built by the L.M.S. in 1932. Withdrawn 1955.   **p. 310**

47190, 47191

Sentinel locomotives built in 1929 for the S.D.J.R. and acquired in 1930 by the L.M.S. Withdrawn 1959 and 1961.   **p. 310**

47200–47259

Johnson 0–6–0T's built between 1899 and 1902 for the Midland. All eventually rebuilt with Belpaire fireboxes. Withdrawn 1953–66.   **p. 311**

Between **47260** & **47681**

L.M.S. standard design of 0–6–0T shunting engine, a development of the M.R. 7200 class (see upper illustration, page 311). Built between 1924 and 1931; 47310–47316 were originally constructed for the S.D.J.R. Nos. 7456, 7553, 7613, 7617 and 7663 were sold out of service before Nationalisation and never became B.R. stock. The rest were withdrawn 1959–67. Nos. 47327, 47357, 47383, 47445, 47493 and 47564 have been preserved.   **p. 312**

47862, 47865

Two surviving L.N.W.R. 0–4–2PT's of which 20 were built 1896–1901. No. 47865 was scrapped in 1953; No. 47862 in 1956.   **p. 312**

Between **47875** & **47896**

Nine survivors of a class of L.N.W.R. 0–8–2T heavy shunting engines, 30 of which were built between 1911 and 1917. All of them were withdrawn by 1953.   **p. 313**

Between **47930** & **47959**

14 surviving engines of a class of 30 L.N.W.R. design 0-8-4T's, enlargements of the previous class, but not actually built until after the amalgamation in 1923. All scrapped by 1951. **p. 313**

47967–47999

L.M.S. Garratt's for heavy freight working, built by Beyer, Peacock & Co. in 1927–30. All scrapped between 1955 and 1958. **p. 314**

Between **48000** & **48775**

663 2-8-0 locomotives of L.M.S. design originally turned out from Crewe in 1935, but during the war years large numbers were produced not only by outside builders but also by the L.N.E.R., G.W.R., and S.R. from their own works. Some of them actually ran as L.N.E.R. engines with L.N.E.R. numbers for a time, but all were later absorbed in the one L.M.S. series. Nos. 48773–48775 were not taken into stock until 1957, having previously been the property of the War Department. One hundred and fifty still in service at the beginning of 1968, when they were finally withdrawn. No. 48431 and 48774 (with original number L.M.S. 8233) have been preserved. **pp. 315–6**

48801, 48824, 48834

Three survivors of a class of 170 engines, L.N.W.R. 19″ mixed traffic locomotives built between 1906 and 1909. All scrapped by 1950. **p. 316**

Between **48892** & **49454**

L.N.W.R. class 6F and 7F 0-8-0's, originally consisting of 502 engines. Many were rebuilds of earlier classes, some being originally 3- or 4-cylinder compounds, but as modified all presented the same general appearance, the various dimensional differences being practically indistinguishable visually. They were built 1901–18 and 1921–2 and about 275 were still running in 1955, but after that withdrawals were heavy and by the beginning of 1964 there were only five surviving engines, and these were withdrawn later that year. No. 49395 has been preserved. **p. 317**

49500–49674

175 Fowler 0-8-0's constructed between 1929 and 1932. Scrapping commenced in 1949 and by 1962 all had gone. **p. 318**

Between **50412** & **50455**

Seven engines remaining of a class of 75 L. & Y.R. 4–6–0's of Hughes' design built between 1908 and 1925. All withdrawn by 1951. **p. 319**

50617

L. & Y.R. rail motor, combined engine and coach, the last survivor of a class of 18 units, built between 1906 and 1911. Withdrawn in 1948 as 10617. **p. 319**

Between **50621** & **50899**

L. & Y.R. class 2 2–4–2T's (see also No. 46762), built between 1889 and 1910 to the designs of Aspinall and perpetuated by Hoy and Hughes. 110 engines came into B.R. stock in 1948, but by 1962 all had been scrapped. No. 50621 has been restored to its original condition for preservation as L. & Y.R. No. 1008. **p. 320**

Between **50835** & **50953**

Superheated class 3 version of the above, some rebuilt from previous class and others built new in 1911. 14 of the class were taken over by B.R., the last survivor (No. 50925) being scrapped in 1952. **p. 320**

Between **51202** & **51253**

L. & Y.R. Aspinall 0–4–0ST's, built between 1891 and 1910, of which 23 engines remained in service in 1948. No further withdrawals took place before 1956. All had gone by 1964, and Nos. 51218 and 51243 have been preserved.

p. 321

Between **51304** & **51530**

Barton Wright 0–6–0ST's, originally 230 in number, built as 0–6–0 tender engines (see lower illustration, page 321) between 1876 and 1885, and later rebuilt between 1891 and 1900 in their present form. 101 were in service on Nationalisation, but only Nos. 11305, 11324 and 11368, retaining their L.M.S. numbers, were still running in 1963 as works shunters at Horwich. After the withdrawal of the last Johnson goods in January 1964 (see page 74), No. 11305, built in 1877, was for a short time the oldest engine on British Railways, which honour then passed to No. 41708 (see page 61). No. 11456, which was sold out of service, has been preserved. Restored as L. & Y.R. 752. **p. 321**

68

Between **51535** & **51546**

Aspinall 0–6–0T's, originally a class of 20 engines built in 1897. Five survived in 1948, and No. 51537, scrapped in 1961, was the last survivor.   **p. 322**

Between **52016** & **52064**

Barton Wright 0–6–0's, a class of 50 engines built in 1887. They were similar to the class of 230 engines (between Nos. 51304 and 51530); as originally built 25 of these engines came into B.R. stock. The last survivor, No. 52044, which was withdrawn in 1959, has been preserved. Restored as L. & Y.R. 957.   **p. 322**

Between **52088** & **52467** and **52515** & **52529**

Aspinall's standard L. & Y.R. 0–6–0, built in large numbers between 1889 and 1917. There were 246 survivors in 1948 and 70 still running early in 1960. No. 52322 has been restored under private ownership as L. & Y.R. No. 1122. All the rest had gone by 1963.   **p. 323**

Between **52494** & **52510**

Furness Railway 0–6–0's, designed by Pettigrew, built 1913–20. Six engines came in B.R. stock and three of them survived until 1957.   **p. 324**

Between **52541** & **52619**

Hughes' superheated class 3 0–6–0. 20 built new in 1912 and 63 further engines rebuilt from Aspinall design (see page 323). 36 engines were taken over by B.R., but all were scrapped by 1957.   **p. 325**

52727

Aspinall small boilered 0–8–0, a class of 130 engines built 1900–8, 60 of which were never rebuilt. Withdrawn 1950.   **p. 325**

Between **52782** & **52971**

Hughes' large boilered 0–8–0's; some built new from 1910 onwards and others rebuilt from previous class. The later engines were superheated, but all presented the same general appearance. In 1948 28 engines were taken into service by B.R., the last of the class being withdrawn in 1951.   **p. 326**

53800–53810

S.D.J.R. 2–8–0's, designed by Fowler, the first six being built at Derby in 1914. The later enlarged class of five engines was constructed in 1925, but latterly all of these received the smaller boilers similar to Nos. 53800–53805. No. 53800 was broken up in 1959 and the other engines of the earlier series by 1962. Nos. 53806–53810 were withdrawn during 1963–4, but No. 53808 has been preserved.

p. 327

54363 & between **54434** & **54460**

Caledonian McIntosh Dunalastair class 4–4–0's. 22 engines built 1910–14 and two survivors of earlier classes. No. 54363 was unsuperheated, but similar in general appearance. All withdrawn by 1957. **p. 328**

54461–54508

C.R. Pickersgill 4–4–0's, built 1916–22. No. 54481 was broken up in 1953 after being involved in a collision. No further withdrawals took place until 1959, but the entire class had gone by 1962. **p. 328**

54379, 54385

Highland Railway Loch class (rebuilt with C.R. boilers), two survivors of a class of 18 engines built 1896–1917. Both engines were scrapped by 1950 without being renumbered. **p. 329**

Between **54397** & **54416**

Highland Small Ben class consisting of 20 engines constructed between 1898 and 1906. Ten came into B.R. stock, but all were withdrawn by 1953. No. 54398 *Ben Alder* was still in existence in 1964 with hopes of preservation, but regrettably these did not materialise. **pp. 329–30**

Between **54630** & **54655**

Pickersgill 60 class 4–6–0's. Nos. 54650–54655 built by Caledonian in 1916 and Nos. 54630–54649 by L.M.S. in 1925–6. British Railways took over 23 engines, the last survivor being withdrawn in 1953. **p. 330**

54764, 54767

H.R. Clan class, originally eight engines built 1918–21. Both withdrawn by 1950, No. 14764 without being renumbered. **p. 331**

Between **55116** & **55124**

Original Caledonian McIntosh 0–4–4T design with small side tanks, built 1895
Seven engines in service by 1948; all scrapped by 1953 except No. 55124, which
was in service until 1961 and not finally broken up until 1963. **p. 331**

Between **55125** & **55146**

McIntosh 1897 design 0–4–4T with enlarged side tanks, built 1897–1900.
19 engines existed in 1948 and No. 55126, the last survivor, was scrapped in
1961. All originally fitted with condensing apparatus, as in the engine illustrated,
but later removed in some cases. **p. 332**

Between **55159** & **55240, 55260** & **55269**

Similar to previous class, but non-condensing and with other slight modifications,
although almost identical in appearance. Construction continued by C.R. from
1900–22 and ten further engines built by L.M.S. in 1925. Two engines scrapped
before 1948, but about 55 still running at the beginning of 1960. These were all
withdrawn by 1963. No. 55189 has been preserved, restored as C.R. 419. **p. 332**

55051, 55053

Originally a class of four 0–4–4T engines built by the H.R., 1905–6. Both
scrapped in 1956–7. **p. 333**

Between **55350** & **55361**

Caledonian Pickersgill 4–6–2T's, built 1917. Ten engines absorbed into B.R. in
1948, the last of the class being scrapped in 1953. **p. 333**

Between **56010** & **56039**

C.R. 'Pug' tanks, designed by Dugald Drummond and built 1878–1908.
14 engines running in 1948; seven still in service in 1959, but all had gone by
1963. **p. 334**

56151–56173

C.R. dock tanks, built 1911–21. All were withdrawn between 1958 and 1961.
p. 335

56230–56376

McIntosh standard shunting 0–6–0T's, built between 1905 and 1922. All came into B.R. stock. Withdrawal commenced in 1952; 30 were still in service early in 1961, but all had gone by 1963. **pp. 335–6**

56905

G. & S.W.R. 0–6–2T, last survivor of 28 engines built 1915–19. Withdrawn 1948 as No. 16905. **p. 336**

Between 57230 & 57473

Caledonian standard 0–6–0 Jumbo, built 1883–97 by Drummond, Lambie and McIntosh. 238 engines in service in 1948; over 100 still running in 1961, reduced to less than 20 by 1963, and all of these were withdrawn by 1964. **p. 337**

Between 57550 & 57645

McIntosh class 3 0–6–0's, built 1899–1909. 93 locomotives were taken over by B.R.; 65 were in service in 1961, but only about a dozen remained by 1963 and all had gone by 1964. No. 57566 has been preserved, restored as C.R. 828. **p. 338**

Between 57650 & 57692

Pickersgill 0–6–0's, originally built 1918 and 1920. 29 engines came into B.R. stock on Nationalisation, nearly all still running in 1961, but less than 12 remained in 1963 and these were scrapped by 1964. **p. 338**

Between 57693 & 57702

Highland Railway 'Barney' 0–6–0's. Originally a class of 12 engines, built 1900–7, of which seven came into B.R. stock, but all were scrapped by 1952. **pp. 339–40**

57950/1, 57953–57956

H.R. Clan Goods, built 1917–19. A class of eight engines, six surviving in 1948 and the last survivor scrapped in 1952. **p. 340**

58000–58003

L.N.W.R. Prince of Wales class 4–6–0's. A once numerous class of 246 engines built 1911–24. None of these engines survived to carry their new B.R. allocated numbers and all were scrapped by 1949 under their L.M.S. numbers, 25648, 25673, 25752 and 25787. **p. 341**

58010

L.N.W.R. Precursor class 4–4–0. One surviving engine of a class of 130 loco-motives built 1904–7. The engine had been rebuilt with superheater and Belpaire firebox. It was scrapped in 1949 as L.M.S. No. 25297. **p. 342**

58011, 58012

L.N.W.R. George V class 4–4–0's. Nos. 25350 and 25373 were the last two surviving engines of a class of 90 built 1910–15. A third engine, No. 25321, actually lasted until February 1948, but was not included in the renumbering scheme. Neither of the survivors carried its B.R. number, both being scrapped in 1948. **p. 342**

58020

Midland Johnson 6'3" 2–4–0. The sole survivor of a class of ten engines built in 1876. This locomotive was later rebuilt with Belpaire firebox. Scrapped 1950 as L.M.S. No. 20155. **p. 343**

58021

M.R. Johnson 6'6" 2–4–0. One survivor (rebuilt with Belpaire firebox) of a class of 40 engines built in 1876. Scrapped 1948 as L.M.S. No. 20185. **p. 343**

58022

Midland Johnson 6'9" 2–4–0. One locomotive, a rebuild with Belpaire firebox, of a class of 65 engines built 1879–81, remained in 1948. Scrapped 1949 as L.M.S. No. 20216. **p. 344**

58092

L.N.W.R. 2–4–0T. The only surviving engine of a class of 18, built 1876–85, was scrapped in 1952. **p. 344**

58030–58038

Midland Johnson 5'7" 0–4–4T's, built 1875–6. The last engine of this class was scrapped in 1954. **p. 345**

58039–58091

M.R. Johnson 5'3" 0–4–4T's. Originally 165 engines, built between 1881 and 1900. No. 58086, the last of the class, was scrapped in 1960. **p. 346**

73

58100

Midland 0–10–0 banking engine, built in 1919, the only one of its class. It was withdrawn from service in 1956. **p. 347**

58110

Midland Railway Kirtley 0–6–0 with Johnson boiler. This engine, together with Nos. 58111–58113, were the last survivors of a class once numbering several hundred engines built between 1863 and 1874. Scrapped 1951. **p. 347**

58111–58113

M.R. Kirtley 0–6–0's rebuilt with Belpaire boilers. They were rebuilt from the previous class. The last engine was scrapped in 1950; none carried their allocated B.R. numbers. **p. 348**

58114–58228, 58249–58310

Johnson class 2 5'3" 0–6–0's, built between 1875 and 1902. Nearly all were rebuilt with Belpaire boilers, but there were one or two engines with Johnson boilers in 1948 similar to that depicted in the illustration of No. 58236 (see page 350). These engines, together with the variants shown in these pages, formed part of a large class of M.R. engines, originally totalling 865. About half of them, mainly the later built ones, were subsequently provided with class 3 boilers (at first non-Belpaire, later Belpaire) and constituted the class in the series 43174–43763. All of the surviving class 2 engines, which formerly bore L.M.S. numbers between 22900 and 23018, and 3023 and 3764, were renumbered under Nationalisation into the present 58114–58310 group. Several of the earliest 1875 to 1877 group still survived in 1959, and as such they represented the oldest class of locomotives still running in any considerable numbers. About 30 engines of the class were still in service in 1961, but by 1963 only Nos. 58143, 58148 and 58182 were still running. The last survivor of all, No. 58182, went in January 1964, at which time it was the oldest running locomotive on British Railways, having been built in 1876. **pp. 348–9**

58229–58248

Johnson class 2 0–6–0's, similar to the previous class but with 4'11" wheels, built 1885–8. The last survivor was taken out of traffic in 1959. **p. 350**

58320–58361

L.N.W.R. Webb 'Coal Engine', originally a class of 500 locomotives built between 1873 and 1892. The L.M.S. numbers of the engines transferred to B.R. ranged from 28088 to 28313. All were broken up by 1953. **p. 351**

58362–58430

L.N.W.R. Webb 18″ goods, usually known by the nickname 'Cauliflower'. This class of 310 engines was built between 1880 and 1902. Scrapping commenced in 1918, and the last survivors ran until 1955. **p. 352**

58850–58863

N.L.R. 0–6–0T's, originally a class of 30 engines built between 1887 and 1905. Late L.M.S. numbers ranged from 27505 and 27532. Only No. 58850 remained early in 1960, and this engine has been preserved, restored as L.N.W.R. No. 2650. **p. 353**

58865

North London 0–4–2ST crane engine, built in 1858, and the oldest engine to come into the stock of British Railways. It was withdrawn from service in 1951. **p. 354**

58870

L.N.W.R. 0–6–0PT, sole survivor of a class of 45 engines. Originally built as 0–6–0 tender engines and later rebuilt with square saddle tanks from 1904 to 1907. Scrapped 1948 as L.M.S. No. 27480. **p. 354**

58880–58937

L.N.W.R. Webb 4′5½″ 0–6–2T's, familiarly known as 'Coal Tanks'. Between the years 1881 and 1896, 300 of the class were built. L.M.S. numbers ranged from 27553 to 27681 and between 7682 and 7841. All were scrapped by 1955, except No. 58926, which was not taken out of service until 1958. It has now been preserved as L.N.W.R. No. 1054. **p. 355**

Service locomotives 3, 6, 7, 8, 3323

L.N.W.R. 0–6–0ST (Special Tank). These were built in large numbers from 1870 onwards, but the only remaining engines in 1948 were employed in Departmental duties. All were scrapped between 1957 and 1959. **p. 356**

Narrow gauge service locomotive *Wren*

The last survivor of eight engines built between 1887 and 1901 for the 18″ gauge works system at Horwich. Since its withdrawal in 1962 it has been preserved, painted in L. & Y.R. livery. **p. 357**

75

Rail motor

L.N.W.R. rail motor car, combined engine and coach. The last survivor of six units built 1905–6 and scrapped in 1948. **p. 357**

103

Highland Railway 'Jones Goods', the first 4–6–0 in the British Isles. 15 engines, Nos. 103–117, were built in 1894. They later became L.M.S. Nos. 17916–17930 and were withdrawn between 1929 and 1940. The original engine, however, was preserved, at first in Highland Railway green, but in 1959 it was restored to working order and repainted in Stroudley yellow, a livery in use on the Highland during the 1870s and 1880s. No. 103 is understood to have run in this colour for a time when it was first built, although the official livery was by then olive green. Preserved as a static exhibit. **p. 358**

123

Caledonian Railway 4–2–2, built by Neilson and Co. in 1886 and took part in the Race to the North two years later. It later became Caledonian Railway No. 1123 and subsequently L.M.S. No. 14010. Withdrawn in 1935, it was repainted in Caledonian colours and restored to working order in 1959. Preserved as a static exhibit. **p. 358**

THE LNER GROUP

The L.N.E.R. Group

At Nationalisation the London & North Eastern Railway possessed some 6,550 steam locomotives of about 150 main classes, many of which embraced several variations of major or minor importance.

Variations are particularly numerous in this group, there being considerably more than are to be found on the other three major systems, and these embrace such details as size and shape of the various boiler mountings, chimneys and, in particular, domes, different designs of tender carried by engines of the same class, fitting of Westinghouse in addition to, or in place of, vacuum brakes, adaption for pull-and-push working, and so on. In a very few cases the reverse holds true, in that two separate classes, where the differences may not be visible externally (for example classes N4 and N5, which are only distinguished by possessing different forms of internal valve gear), are to outward appearances identical and can therefore be covered by one illustration.

In 1946, only two years before Nationalisation, the locomotive stock of the L.N.E.R. had been completely renumbered. Previous to that time the engines of each of the pre-grouping constituent companies were fairly easily identifiable by their numbers, after allowing for the fact that many blanks in the list below 5000 had been filled in by new post-grouping construction. North Eastern engines had retained their old numbers, which ran up to 2404, followed by the absorbed Hull & Barnsley stock. Great Northern locomotives had their old numbers increased by 3000 (and consequently became 3001 upwards). Great Central engines commenced at 5001, Great North of Scotland at 6801, Great Eastern at 7001 and North British at 9001. Whilst this method had the advantage of preserving the identity of the individual engines, there was at the same time very little else to recommend it, as many classes of engine were in no sort of sequence and their numbers could be found scattered almost indiscriminately throughout the list. This was particularly so with the old North Eastern locomotives.

Under the 1946 scheme the whole stock was renumbered according to class in an orderly and systematic manner between 1 and 10000. Similar types from the various companies were placed together, the larger passenger engines coming first, followed by mixed traffic and freight engines, with tank engines coming at the end of the list. Generally speaking, also, each class was renumbered in the correct order in which the individual engines had been built, although for some reason the plan was not followed with the Gresley 'Pacifics'.

. This general renumbering resulted in each class becoming a complete entity and greatly simplifies the layout of this section. L.N.E.R. engines, with the one solitary exception of No. 10000, which became 60700, had 60000 added to their existing numbers at Nationalisation, after a short period during which the prefix 'E' was in use, and consequently the various classes still fell in compact groups of blocks of numbers.

During the twenty-five years of its existence, the L.N.E.R. had not gone in for standardisation to the extent of the L.M.S. and Great Western companies. Consequently at the end of the Second World War there was to be found on their line, not only a much greater proportion of pre-grouping engines still in existence, but the number of classes, some of them consisting of a comparatively small total of locomotives, was much more numerous. Whilst this was a great advantage from the interest point of view, it was not so favourable from an operating and maintenance standpoint. Steps were being taken by the L.N.E.R. to remedy this state of affairs, notably by the construction of large numbers of standard general purpose B1 class 4–6–0's, whose appearance played havoc with many of the older passenger classes, particularly the 'Atlantics' of the Great Northern, North Eastern and Great Central Railways, and also the several classes of 4–6–0's formerly owned by the latter company. Several of these types, such as the G.C.R. 'Lord Faringdon' and compound 'Atlantics', disappeared during the year 1947 and thus unfortunately just failed to qualify for incorporation in this volume.

The only new engines of L.N.E.R. design to be constructed subsequent to absorption were a series of 6'8" 'Pacifics' built by Mr. A. H. Peppercorn, Nos. 60114–60161, all of which followed the design of the reconstructed 60113, *Great Northern*; the completion of a series of 6'2" 'Pacifics', Nos. 60527–60539; a batch of 70 2–6–0's of class K1, again the continuation of a prototype reconstruction; the finishing of an order of 100 2–6–4T's of class L1; some further B1 class 4–6–0's; finally a series of small 0–6–0T engines which were remarkable in being not only of pre-Nationalisation design, but actually of a pre-grouping design of the North Eastern dating back to 1898. They were, moreover, exact replicas of the original engines, with no modification of any sort. All of the above types had been ordered by the L.N.E.R. and no further locomotives were constructed to L.N.E.R. design.

By mid-1967 only a few engines of L.N.E.R. origin and design remained, these being mainly Thompson B1 4–6–0's and Peppercorn 2–6–0's of class K1 (all built after Nationalisation). However, the old North Eastern and North British Railways shared the honour of having provided the last pre-grouping engines to remain in regular service, the J36 and J37 0–6–0's of the N.B.R. and the J27 0–6–0's and Q6 0–8–0's of the North Eastern, although there was also a narrow gauge 2–6–2T of Cambrian origin (see page 14).

Class List - Historical Data
List of Illustrations

60001–60034

Class A4 Gresley streamlined 'Pacifics'. The original four engines (now 60014–60017) were introduced in 1935 for working the 'Silver Jubilee', Britain's first high-speed completely streamlined train. Additional engines were completed 1936–8 for other similar services and for general main line work. No. 60022, *Mallard*, holds the world's highest authenticated speed for steam, $126\frac{1}{2}$ m.p.h., attained on a test run on 7 July, 1938. All withdrawn 1963–6. Six engines have been preserved, some in working order: Nos. 60022 and 60007 (as L.N.E.R. 4468 and 4498), 60019 (as L.N.E.R. 19) and 60009, plus 60008 and 60010, which are in the U.S.A. and Canada respectively. **p. 361**

60035–60112

Class A3 Gresley 'Pacifics', originally introduced 1922, the first two engines coming out under Great Northern ownership. The earlier engines of the series had 180 lbs. pressure, but all have since been rebuilt with 220 lbs. pressure in line with the later development of the class, first introduced in 1927. No. 60104 was withdrawn in December 1959, and all had gone by 1965. No. 60103 *Flying Scotsman* has been restored as L.N.E.R. 4472, in working order. It spent several years in America but has now returned to the U.K. and will be used on steam specials. **pp. 362–3**

60113

Class A1/1. The original Gresley 'Pacific', formerly No. 4470, completely rebuilt in 1945 as the class A1 prototype. Withdrawn in 1962. **p. 364**

60114–60162

Class A1, a slightly modified version of class A1/1, built by Mr. A. H. Peppercorn in 1948 and 1949. 6'8" wheels, 3 cylinders. All withdrawn 1962–6. **p. 365**

60500, 60511–60524

Class A2/3, Thompson 6'2" 'Pacifics', built 1946–7, 3 cylinders. All withdrawn 1962–5. **p. 366**

60501–60506

Class A2/2, originally built in 1934–6 as 2–8–2's for service between Edinburgh and Aberdeen. Rebuilt 1943–4 by Thompson as 'Pacifics'. 6'2" wheels, 3 cylinders. All were withdrawn from 1959–61. No. 60532 has been preserved as L.N.E.R. 532. **p. 366**

60507–60510

Class A2/1, 6'2" 'Pacifics', built 1944, a development of V2 class (see 60800) with leading bogie, 3 cylinders. All withdrawn 1960–1. **p. 367**

60525–60539

Class A2 Peppercorn 6'2" 'Pacifics', a development of class A2/3 built between 1947–8. 3 cylinders. All withdrawn 1962–6. **p. 367**

60700

Class W1, originally L.N.E.R. No. 10000. Gresley's 4-cylinder compound with water-tube boiler built in 1929. Rebuilt in 1937 with three cylinders. It was scrapped in 1959. **p. 368**

60800–60983

Class V2, Gresley's 'Green Arrow' class 2–6–2's, introduced in 1936 for mixed traffic duties, but used largely on express main line work. 6'2" wheels, 3 cylinders. All withdrawn 1962–6. The original engine, No. 60800, has been preserved, restored as L.N.E.R. 4771 *Green Arrow*, in working order. **p. 368**

61000–61409

Class B1. Thompson general purpose 2-cylinder 4–6–0's with 6'2" wheels built 1942–50. They replaced G.N.R., G.C.R., and N.E.R. 'Atlantics', various G.C.R. 4–6–0 classes, and 4–4–0's from all of the constituent L.N.E.R. companies. No. 61057 was scrapped in 1950 after a collision at Chelmsford. Scrapping on a considerable scale began in 1962 but was not completed until 1967, this being one of the last L.N.E.R. classes to remain in service. No. 61306 has been preserved in L.N.E.R. livery with the name *Mayflower*, formerly carried by No. 61379. **p. 369**

82

61353/4/5/7/8

Class B8, originally 11 engines. Robinson's 'Glenalmond' mixed express freight engines built for the Great Central 1913–15. 5'7" wheels. All scrapped between 1947 and 1949. **p. 369**

61360–61397

Class B7, Robinson 4-cylinder mixed traffics with 5'7" wheels, built 1921–4. All of the class were scrapped between 1948 and 1950. None carried a 61300 number, but in 1949 the last survivors, Nos. 1365/7, 1375/7, 1381/2/6/7/8, 1391/2/6, were allocated new numbers 61702–61713 to make way for the new B1 class 4–6–0's, then under construction (see previous page), and some of them actually carried these numbers for a short time before being scrapped. **p. 370**

61400–61468

Classes B16, B16/2, B16/3. North Eastern 3-cylinder mixed traffic 4–6–0's, built 1919–24 with 5'8" wheels. Originally a class of 70 engines, one of which was destroyed in an air raid. In 1949 the first ten were renumbered 61469–61478 in consequence of the construction of further B1's, by which time class B9 had become extinct. Classes B16/2 and B16/3 were rebuilds of class B16 with Walschaert's gear and higher running plates. 24 of the class were rebuilt in this form. The earlier rebuilds, dating from 1937, had Gresley's double Walschaert gear and derived motion from the inside cylinder. Those altered by Thompson from 1944 onwards had three independent Walschaert gears. With-drawal commenced in 1958 and the last survivors went in 1964. **p. 371**

61469, 61470/5/6

Class B9, Robinson's Great Central 5'3" express freight engines with 2 cylinders. Ten engines built in 1906; all scrapped by 1949. **p. 372**

61482/3/5/8

Class B4, or 'Imminghams', a Great Central class of ten engines built in 1906 with 6'7" wheels. All of the class were scrapped 1944–9. **p. 372**

61497

Class B3/3. The survivor of Robinson's 6'9" 4-cylinder 'Lord Faringdon' class, built 1917–20. All were withdrawn 1946–7, except No. 1497, which had been completely rebuilt in 1942 as a 2-cylinder engine. Scrapped in 1949. **p. 373**

61680/1/5/6/8/9, 61690

Class B5, Robinson's 6'1" 2-cylinder 4–6–0's. A class of 14 engines, built 1902–4 and colloquially known as the 'Fish' class. All of the class scrapped by 1950. **p. 373**

61500–61580

Classes B12 and B12/3. Holden Great Eastern 4–6–0's, originally built 1911–20 with 6'6" wheels. Many were rebuilt to class B12/3. Most of the unconverted engines were transferred to the Great North of Scotland section from 1931 onwards, where they remained for the rest of their existence, the last of them being withdrawn in November 1954. The last ten engines, Nos. 61571–61580, were built new in 1928 with raised running plates over the wheels and valve modifications. From 1932 onwards many of the class were rebuilt by Gresley with larger round-topped boilers, piston valves and the footplating raised, as in Nos. 61571–61580. These rebuilt engines were reclassified B12/3 and only No. 61572 remained in 1961. This engine has been preserved. **pp. 374–5**

61699

Class B13. Sole survivor of a class of 40 6'1¼" 4–6–0's built between 1899 and 1909 for the North Eastern Railway. This engine was withdrawn from ordinary traffic in 1934 and used as a counter-pressure locomotive for testing purposes at Darlington and later at Rugby. It was scrapped in 1951 as No. 1699. **p. 375**

61600–61672

Classes B17 and B2. Gresley's 'Sandringham' 3-cylinder 4–6–0's, built 1928–37 as class B17, with 6'8" wheels and three cylinders. After 1945 a number of these locomotives were rebuilt as class B2 with two cylinders and B1-type boilers, which were also carried by some of the unconverted 3-cylinder engines. This class was found with varying types of tenders of G.E.R., N.E.R. and L.N.E.R. origin. In 1937 two of the class, Nos. 61659 and 61670, were streamlined similar to the A4 'Pacifics' for working the 'East Anglian' between London and Norwich. In this form they were classified B17/5. The streamlining was removed in 1951 and the engines became class B17/6, the subdivision of the class as applied to those locomotives carrying the B1-type boiler. Wholesale withdrawal took place in 1958–9, and all of the class had gone by 1960. **pp. 376–7**

61700, 61701

Class V4, Gresley's last design, introduced in 1944. Lightweight mixed traffic 2–6–2's, they were intended as a prototype of a new general purpose engine, but were superseded by Thompson's B1 class of 1942. 5'8" wheels, 3 cylinders. Both scrapped in 1957. **p. 377**

61720–61794

Class K2. Gresley 5'8" 2-cylinder 2–6–0's, built 1912–21. After 1925 a number of the class were transferred to Scotland and received side window cabs, most of them at the same time being named after lochs. Scrapping commenced in 1955, and by 1963 all locomotives of this class had gone.   **p. 378**

61800–61992

Class K3. Gresley 5'8" 3-cylinder locomotives with larger 6'0" boilers. Built between 1920 and 1937. No. 61863 was rebuilt in 1945 with two cylinders and reclassified K5. All were withdrawn 1959–62.   **p. 379**

61993–61998

Class K4. Gresley 5'2" 3-cylinder engines for the West Highland line, built 1937–8. No. 61997 was rebuilt by Thompson in 1945 with 2 cylinders and re-classified K1, forming the prototype for the new series commencing 62001 built in 1949–50. All were withdrawn by 1961, but No. 61994 has been preserved in original L.N.E.R. livery as No. 3442 *The Great Marquess*.   **p. 380**

62001–62070

Class K1. Peppercorn development of rebuilt engine No. 61997. Scrapping commenced in 1962, but was not completed until 1967, this being one of the last L.N.E.R. designed classes to remain at work. No. 62005 has been preserved.
                    p. 381

62059, 62060/2/4–6, 62072

Class D31. North British 6'6" 4–4–0's, originally 48 engines of three classes designed by Holmes, built 1884–99, and subsequently rebuilt into one class. The last seven survivors were scrapped in 1952. To make way for the new class K1 engines built in 1949–50, the last three remaining locomotives, Nos. 62059, 62060 and 62072, were renumbered 62281–62283.   **p. 381**

62111, 62112

Class D17. Worsdell 7'1¼" 4–4–0's, originally North Eastern class Q of 30 engines built 1896–7. These last two of the class were withdrawn in 1948 as Nos. 2111 and 2112.   **p. 382**

62000

Class D3, G.N.R. Ivatt 6'8" 4–4–0, built 1897. Formerly L.N.E.R. No. 4075, it was modified in 1944 for working officers' saloons, repainted green and renumbered 2000. For a short time it carried the number 1. Scrapped in 1951.

p. 382

62116, 62122–6/8, 62132/3/5/7/9, 62140/3/4/5/8

Class D3. G.N.R. Ivatt 4–4–0's originally a class of 51 engines built between 1896 and 1899. Nos. 2143–3148 had raised running plates over the coupling rods and were very similar in appearance to classes D1 and D2. All scrapped by 1951.

p. 383

62150–7, 62150/1/3/5/7/9, 62172/3/5/7/9, 62180/1/7–9, 62190/3–5/7–9, 62203/ 5/7–9, 62214/5

Classes D1 and D2. G.N.R. Ivatt 6'8" 4–4–0's, built 1898–1909 (class D2), and 1911 (class D1, Nos. 62203 upwards). In the two classes there were originally 85 locomotives. Some class D2 engines were superheated and as such were similar in appearance to the slightly more powerful D1's. Nos. 62150 and 62152–62154 had flat running plates and resembled class D3. Class D1 engines were dual fitted with Westinghouse in addition to vacuum brakes. All were scrapped by 1951.

p. 384

62225/7–32/4/5/8, 62240–3/6–9, 62251/2/5/6

Class D41, Great North of Scotland 6'1" 4–4–0's designed by James Johnson and built 1893–8. There were originally 32 engines in the class, of which 22 survived into 1948; the last was scrapped in 1953. **p. 385**

62260–2/4/5/7–79

Class D40. G.N.S.R. Pickersgill 6'1" 4–4–0's, originally 21 engines built between 1899 and 1920. The last eight, turned out in 1920, had superheaters and extended smokeboxes, while one or two of the earlier engines were rebuilt in this manner. No. 62277 survived until 1959, when it was restored to its original condition, in working order, as G.N.S.R. No. 49 *Gordon Highlander*. Now preserved as a static museum exhibit. **pp. 385–6**

62300–9, 62311–5/7/9, 62321/2/4/5/9, 62330/2/3

Class D9. Great Central 6'9" 4–4–0's, a class of 40 engines built by Robinson between 1901 and 1904 and later rebuilt with larger boilers. Of the 26 survivors to come into British Railways' stock, all were withdrawn by 1950. **p. 387**

86

62340–5/7–9, 62351–5/7–63/5–7, 62369–84, 62386–92/5–7

Class D20. North Eastern class R 4–4–0's with 6'10" wheels, designed by W. Worsdell and later superheated. Originally 60 engines in the class built between 1899–1907. The last of the class disappeared in 1957. **pp. 387–8**

62400–6, 62409–13

Class D29, the earlier 'Scott' series of the North British Railway, 6'6" 4–4–0's. Originally 16 engines in the class, built 1909–11 and subsequently superheated. Last of the class was scrapped 1952. **p. 389**

62417–32, 62434–42

Class D30, the later 'Scott' series of 27 engines in the class, built new with superheaters between 1912 and 1920. Two engines had been scrapped prior to Nationalisation, and from 1957 onwards the remainder began to be taken out of service. All had gone by 1960. **p. 389**

62443–6/8–51/3/4

Class D32, originally class K of the North British Railway. Originally consisting of 12 locomotives (4–4–0's with 6'0" driving wheels), they were also known as the 'Intermediates'. Built in 1906, they were all scrapped by 1951. **p. 390**

62455/7–64/6

Class D33 of 12 engines built 1909–10. The last was scrapped in 1953. **p. 390**

62467–85, 62487–90/2–8

Class D34. North British 'Glen' class 6'0" 4–4–0's, consisting of 32 engines built 1913–20. Two of the class were scrapped prior to Nationalisation and general scrapping began in 1959 and was completed by 1962. No. 62469 has been restored, in working condition, as N.B.R. No. 256 *Glen Douglas*; now preserved as a static museum exhibit. **pp. 390–1**

62501–9, 62512, 62520/8, 62538

Class D15 better known as the Great Eastern 'Claud Hamilton' class, 4–4–0's with 7'0" driving wheels. Built 1900–3, the whole class comprising those engines not converted to class D16. They were rebuilt between 1915 and 1931 with Belpaire boilers and all were scrapped by 1952. The original engine, No. 2500, *Claud Hamilton*, which had been converted to class D16/3, was withdrawn in 1947. **pp. 391–2**

62543/7, 62552/3/8, 62564/9, 62570/7, 62580, 62590/1, 62603, 62612/13/20

Class D16/2, or 'Super Clauds', being rebuilds of the 'Claud Hamilton' class with larger boilers and extended smokeboxes. Nos. 62612/3/20 were from the final series of ten built new in 1923 with the large boiler. After 1948 all of these engines were either scrapped, or again converted to class D16/3. No 62590, scrapped in 1952, was the last to run with a Belpaire boiler. **p. 392**

62542/4, 62554/6/7, 62562/5, 62573/8, 62584/9, 62592/6, 62601/5–7, 62611/5/7–9

Class D16/3. 'Claud Hamiltons' rebuilt from 1938 onwards with round-topped boilers, but retaining the original framing. After 1948 the class was augmented by rebuilds from class D16/2. All have now been scrapped (see paragraph below). **p. 393**

62510/1/3–9, 62521–7/9–36/9–41/5/6/8/9, 62551/5/9–61/3/6–8, 62571/2/4–6/9, 62581–3/5–8, 62593/4/7–9

Class D16/3. 'Claud Hamiltons' rebuilt from 1933 onwards with round-topped boilers, modified splashers and framing. Some locomotives of both varieties of D16/3 had piston valves and some slide valves. It is of interest to note that there were originally 121 engines in the 'Claud Hamilton' class, built between 1900 and 1923. Some engines, including the original *Claud Hamilton*, whose name-plate was later carried on engine 62546, were scrapped prior to Nationalisation. Scrapping of these D16/3 engines of both varieties (see paragraph above) took place on a large scale 1957–9, and the last survivor, No. 62613, went in 1960. **p. 393**

62650–62659

Class D10. Great Central Robinson 'Directors', original series, built in 1913 with 6'9" wheels. All withdrawn between 1953 and 1955. **p. 394**

62660–62670

Class D11/1. Enlarged 'Directors', a class of 11 engines built 1920–2. All were withdrawn 1959–60. No. 62660 has been preserved in its original G.C.R. condition as No. 506 *Butler Henderson*. **p. 394**

62671–62694

Class D11/2 consisting of subsequent additions to class D11/1, built in 1924 with cut-down boiler mountings for service in Scotland. Both classes D10 and D11 originally had straight framing and coupling-rod splashers, the latter being later removed and the framing cut away to render the coupling rods more easily accessible. Withdrawal commenced in 1958 and all had gone by 1962. **p. 395**

62700–62725, 62728–62735

Class D49/1. Gresley 3-cylinder 6'8" 4–4–0 passenger engines with Walschaert's valve gear. Named after counties and known as the 'Shire' class. See also next paragraph. **p. 395**

62726, 62727, 62736–62767, 62769–62775

Class D49/2, a variation of the 'Shire' class above, with Lentz poppet valves. Familiarly known as the 'Hunt' class. Scrapping of both 'Shire' and 'Hunt' classes began in 1957 and the last were taken out of service in 1961. **p. 396**

62768

Class D49/4. Formerly class D49/2, but rebuilt in 1942 with two inside cylinders. No other engines of the class were so treated, the solitary example being withdrawn from service in 1952. **p. 396**

62780–62797

Class E4, Great Eastern 5'8" mixed traffic 2–4–0's designed by Holden. There were originally 100 engines in the class built between 1891 and 1902, of which 82 were scrapped between 1926 and 1940. No further withdrawals were made after that date until the close of 1954, when Nos. 62782 and 62783 were taken out of traffic. The remainder followed gradually and the last one, No. 62785, was taken out of service in 1959. This locomotive has however now been preserved as G.E.R. No. 490. **pp. 397–8**

62808, 62810/7, 62821/2/8/9, 62839, 62849, 62854, 62870/1/5–7, 62881/5

Class C1. Ivatt's large Great Northern 'Atlantics' with 2 outside cylinders and 6'8" wheels. A class of originally 93 engines built 1902–10. Of the 17 survivors to come into British Railways' stock, all were taken out of service by 1950, but the original engine has been restored to its original state as G.N.R. No. 251 and preserved. **pp. 398–9**

62900–3, 62908–10, 62912, 62914–25

Class C4. Robinson's Great Central 'Atlantics' with 6'9" wheels and 2 outside cylinders. Originally a class of 27 engines built 1903–6, they were all scrapped by 1950. Four very similar engines were built as compounds, but these all went in 1946–7. **p. 400**

62933, 62937

Class C6. Worsdell 2-cylinder 'Atlantics', 6′10″ wheels, originally North Eastern class V. Ten engines built between 1903 and 1904. Eight engines were scrapped between 1943 and 1947, and the surviving two in 1948. **p. 400**

62954, 62970/2/3/5/8, 62981–3/8/9, 62992/3/5

Class C7. Raven 3-cylinder 'Atlantics' with 6′10″ wheels. Originally North Eastern class Z of 50 engines built 1911–18. Scrapping commenced in 1942, all the British Railways' survivors going in 1948. **p. 401**

63000–63199

Class O7, later renumbered 90000–90100, 90422–90520. War Department Austerity design of 2-8-0, several hundred of which were built between 1943 and 1945, the majority of which went overseas. On return, 200 of them were taken into L.N.E.R. stock in 1947, becoming Nos. 3000–3199. After being at first allocated Nos. 63000–63199, they were later incorporated into the 90000 series, which embraced the whole of the stock coming under British Railways' ownership. See also page 113. **p. 401**

63200–7, 63210–24/6/7/9–21/3–9, 63231–6/8, 63240/1/3

Class Q4, Robinson G.C.R. 0-8-0's, originally 89 engines built 1902–11, with 4′8″ wheels and 2 outside cylinders. Several of the class were superheated and some were fitted with piston valves. The class as a whole was withdrawn from 1934 onwards, the last going in 1951. It is interesting to note that 13 locomotives of this class were rebuilt as tank engines, see Nos. 69925–69937. **p. 402**

63250–2/4–7/9–62/4/7/8, 63270–87, 63289–63300, 63303/7/8, 63310–5/7–9, 63321/3/6–8, 63330–6/8/9

Class Q5. Worsdell 2-cylinder 0-8-0's with 4′7″ wheels. 90 engines in class built 1901–11. All scrapped between 1946 and 1951. **p. 403**

63253, 63263, 63301/5/6, 63316, 63322

Class Q5/2 consisting of class Q5 locomotives rebuilt with larger boilers from Hull & Barnsley 0-8-0's, which had been withdrawn in 1931. The class was finally withdrawn from service by 1949. **p. 403**

63340–63459

Class Q6. Raven 2-cylinder 0-8-0's with 4′7″ wheels, built from 1913–21. Scrapping began in 1960, but a few survived as late as 1967 and, together with some J27 0–6–0's, were the last pre-grouping engines of any railway to remain in regular service. No. 63395 has been preserved, restored as L.N.E.R. 3395.

p. 404

63460–63474

Class Q7. Raven 3-cylinder 0–8–0's with 4'7" wheels. Built between 1919 and 1924. All were withdrawn *en bloc* in December 1962, but the original engine, No. 63460, has been preserved. **p. 404**

63475–86/8/9, 63491/3/4

Class O3. Gresley 2-cylinder G.N.R. 2–8–0's with 4'8" wheels. A class of 20 engines built 1913–19. All of the class were withdrawn between 1947 and 1952.

p. 405

63921

Class O2, the original Gresley 3-cylinder 2–8–0, built in 1918 and the first 3-cylinder locomotive constructed by him. It differed from the rest of the class by having inclined cylinders. Finally withdrawn in 1948 as No. 3921. **p. 405**

63922–63987

Class O2, a development of the original engine (No. 63921). Constructed by Gresley as 3-cylinder 2–8–0's with 4'8" wheels between 1921 and 1934. The whole class was taken out of service between 1960 and 1963. **p. 406**

63571–4/6/7/80/1/3–7/93/7–9, 63601/2/4–9/11/2/4/7/8/20–7/9/31/2/5–42/4/5/7–9, 63654/6–60/4–8/71/2/4/7/9–86/8/90–8, 63700–4/7/9/10/3–24/7–37/9/41–4/6, 63750/1/3/4/6/7/9/62–7/9/71/4/6/8/9/81–3/7/90/1/3/7–9, 63800/1/4/5/7/9/12/3/ 21–3/9, 63832/3/5/7/8, 63840–2/5–7/9/50/2/5/6/8/9/61/2/4, 62870/3/7/8/81/3/5/8/ 9/95/7–9, 63900/2/4–8/11

Classes O4/1, O4/2 and O4/3 Great Central Robinson 4'8" 2–8–0's, built 1911–20. Many of the later ones were built for the Railway Operating Department for service during the First World War and subsequently purchased by the L.N.E.R. between 1924 and 1929. A large number of the class also went overseas during the Second World War (some of them the same engines that saw earlier war service) and these were not returned. Of the 329 locmotives which B.R. took over (including all variations of class O4), five were sold to the War Department in 1952. Some of the unconverted engines were later rebuilt to classes O4/8 and O1 and their numbers consequently appear again in those sections. Withdrawal of all varieties of classes O4 and O1 commenced in 1959 and was completed by 1965. This includes the subdivisions mentioned below. No. 63601 (originally G.C.R. 102) has been preserved. **p. 407**

63913/4/5/7/20

Class O4/6, similar to classes O4/1, O4/2 and O4/3 but fitted with side window cabs. These, plus Nos. 63902 onwards, were built with larger 5′6″ boilers and classified O5, but were later rebuilt with standard 5′0″ boilers in conformity with the rest of the class. **p. 407**

63570/82/8/95/6, 63600/3/15/6, 63634/43/55, 63661/2/9/73/5/99, 63705/6/8/47–9, 63758/61, 63670/2/5/94, 63824/39/43/8, 63857/60/76/80/4/91/4

Class O4/7 rebuilt with G.N.R. O2-type round-topped boiler, but retaining G.C.R. smokebox and chimney. **p. 408**

63628, 63726, 63745/88, 68816/51 (O4/5), 63604/7/13/33/51/3/83, 63703/4/38/50/ 63/85, 63802/7/18/9/27/8/36/53/8/82/93 (O4/8)

Classes O4/5 and O4/8. Class O4/5 had G.N.R. O2-type boiler, smokebox and chimney, while class O4/8 had B1-type boiler (see class O1 below) but retained original cylinders and framing. **p. 408**

63571/8/9, 63589–92/4/6, 63610/9, 63630/36/46/50/2, 63663/70/6/8/87/9, 63711/ 2/25/40/6/52/5/60/8/73/7/80/4/6/9/92/5/6, 63803/6/8/17/38/54/6/63/5/7–9/72/4/ 9/86/7/90, 63901

Class O1. Robinson 2–8–0's rebuilt by Thompson from 1944 onwards with B1 boilers, side window cabs, Walschaert's valve gear and raised running plates.
p. 409

64105–7, 64114–9, 64122–5/7–9, 64131–3/5–7, 64140–2/5/8, 64150–3/8, 64163

Class J3. Stirling and Ivatt 5′2″ 0–6–0 locomotives rebuilt with larger 4′8″ boilers. Nos. 64158 and 64163 were formerly M. & G.N.J.R. Nos. 83 and 88. The last two of the class to remain in service were withdrawn at the end of 1954. **p. 409**

64109, 64110/2, 64120/1, 64160/2/7

Class J4. Stirling and Ivatt 5′2″ 0–6–0's with smaller 4′4″ diameter boilers. No less than 302 were built by the G.N.R. between 1873 and 1901, and 12 more were constructed for the M. & G.N.J.R. in 1900 to the same design. These were absorbed into L.N.E.R. stock in 1937. The Stirling engines originally had dome-less boilers and round-top cabs. Nos. 64160/2/7 were formerly M. & G.N.J.R. Nos. 85, 87 and 92. The last J4, No. 64112, was scrapped in 1951. **p. 410**

64170–64279

Class J6. Ivatt & Gresley 5'2" mixed traffic 0–6–0's, built 1911–22. Scrapping of this class began in 1955 and all had gone by 1963. **p. 411**

64280–64453

Classes J11 and J11/3. Great Central Robinson 5'1" 0–6–0's, built between 1901 and 1910, some of the class being superheated. All the class were in service until 1954, when withdrawals began. Class J11/3 (rebuilt from class J11) have long travel piston valves and higher pitched boilers. 32 of class J11 were so rebuilt between 1942 and 1954. All were withdrawn by 1963. **pp. 411–12**

64460–4/6/8, 64470–80, 64482–64502/4–7, 64509–64535

Class J35. North British Holmes 5'0" 0–6–0's, originally 76 locomotives built 1906–13. Six engines scrapped prior to 1948 and withdrawal was renewed in 1957. All were scrapped by 1963. **p. 412**

64536–64639

Class J37. N.B.R. Reid superheated 5'0" 0–6–0's, a class of 104 engines built between 1914 and 1921. Of the 104 engines in the class, 100 were still in service in 1961 but only about 50 by 1964. The class did not entirely disappear until 1967, amongst the last survivors of the pre-grouping era. **p. 413**

64640–64674

Class J19. Great Eastern 4'11" 0–6–0's designed by Hill and built 1912–20. They were all at first equipped with Belpaire fireboxes, but the whole class was later rebuilt with Gresley round-topped boilers. The whole class was scrapped between 1958 and 1962. **p. 413**

64675–64699

Classes J20 and J20/1, being Hill's larger design of 4'11" 0–6–0's for the G.E.R., built 1920–2 with Belpaire fireboxes. Rebuilding to class J20/1, with Gresley round-topped boilers, commenced in 1943 and all were subsequently converted. All were scrapped between 1959 and 1962. **p. 414**

64700–64988

Class J39. Gresley 5'2" mixed traffic 0–6–0's. A class of 289 engines built 1926–41. They were fitted with several varieties of tenders, some from scrapped North Eastern locomotives. All were withdrawn between 1959 and 1962.

p. 415

65002–10, 65013/4

Class J1. Ivatt mixed traffic 0–6–0's with 5'8" wheels, originally 15 engines built in 1908. Nos. 5000/1, 5011/2 were broken up in 1947, while the last of the class, No. 65013, was scrapped in 1954. Engine No. 5000 was formerly G.N.R. No. 1.
p. 415

65015–65023

Class J2, a larger superheated version of class J1 built in 1912 after Gresley had succeeded Ivatt at Doncaster. Ten engines, wheel diameter 5'8", originally in class, No. 5024 having been scrapped in 1946. The last of the class was withdrawn in 1954.
p. 416

65126–8, 65130–49, 65151/3–73/5–209

Class J10. Parker's design of 0–6–0 for the Manchester, Sheffield and Lincolnshire Railway. There were 124 engines in the class built between 1892 and 1902 (after the formation of the Great Central). Several sizes of tender were fitted to this class. All had gone by 1962.
p. 416

65025–33/5–44/7/9, 65051/2/6–64/6–70, 65072/3/5–84/6/8–95/7–9, 65100–5/7–12/4–23

Class J21. Wordsdell 5'1" 0–6–0's for the N.E.R.; originally 201 engines built between 1886 and 1894, most of which were constructed as compounds, but later constructed as simples, some being superheated. Withdrawn by 1963, but No. 65033 has been preserved.
p. 417

65210/1/3–8, 65220–2/4–61/4–8, 65270/1/3–83/5–98, 65300/3–25/7–31/3–5/7–46

Class J36. North British Holmes 0–6–0's with 5'0" wheels. Originally 168 engines in the class, built 1888–1900. 25 of them served in France during the First World War and on return to this country were given commemorative names, amongst which was No. 65243 *Maude,* which has been preserved. Four were still in service until 1967, amongst the last of any pre-grouping design.   **p. 418**

65350–7/9, 65361–99, 65400–79

Class J15. Great Eastern 4'11" 0–6–0's, an original design by Worsdell in 1883 and perpetuated by J. Holden, S. D. Holden and A. J. Hill to 1913. A number of the class worked overseas in the First World War. No less than 289 engines were built, the first withdrawal taking place in 1920, and of these about 15 were still running in 1961. The last engine to remain in service was withdrawn in 1962. No. 65462 has been preserved as G.E.R. 564.
p. 419

65480–65499

Class J5. G.N.R. Ivatt 0–6–0's with 5'2" wheels, built 1909–10. Nos. 65480 and 65489 were rebuilt with superheaters; all scrapped 1953–5. **p. 420**

65600–4/6–9, 65611/2/4/5/7/9, 65621–9, 65631–4/6/9–42/4

Class J24 North Eastern Worsdell 4'7" 0–6–0's. 70 engines built 1894–8, some of them superheated. All the class were scrapped by 1951. **p. 421**

65645–51, 65653–77, 65679–81, 65683–65700, 65702–8, 65710/2–8, 65720/1/3–8

Class J25, a slightly larger version of class J24 (above). 120 engines built 1898–1902. Both classes were designed purely for freight working and had no continuous brakes. Some were superheated. 10 were still running in 1961, but all had been withdrawn by 1962. **p. 421**

65730–65779

Class J26. Worsdell 4'7" 0–6–0's, a considerably enlarged version of class J24 and 25, with 5'6" boilers as against 4'3" boilers of the two smaller classes. 50 engines were built 1904–5. Withdrawal began in 1958 and all had gone by 1963. **p. 422**

65780–65894

Class J27, a further development of the three preceding classes. 105 engines were built 1906–23. Nos. 65860 onwards, constructed by Sir Vincent Raven, had superheaters and piston valves, but in some instances the superheating elements were removed. Scrapping commenced in 1959, but quite a number survived until 1967. No. 65894 has been preserved, restored as N.E.R. 2392. **p. 422**

65500–65549, 65551–65589

Class J17 G.E.R. Holden 4'11" Belpaire 0–6–0's, built 1900–11. Most of the class originally had round-topped boilers; all were later superheated. 90 engines in the class, the engine that would have become No. 65550 (formerly No. 8200) having been destroyed by a German rocket in 1944. All of the remainder survived until 1954. These were all withdrawn by 1962. No. 65567 has been preserved in its early L.N.E.R. state as No. 1217E. **p. 423**

65900–65934

Class J38. Large 4'8" mineral engines designed by Gresley. A class of 35 engines built in 1926 for use on the North British section in Scotland. Nos. 65923/8

95

were scrapped in 1962; over 25 were still running in 1964. Three of these survived until 1967. **p. 423**

67093/4

Class F7, being the survivors of a class of 12 small 4'10" 2–4–2T's built by S. D. Holden in 1909–10 for the G.E.R. Designed for light branch work, they were known as the 'Crystal Palace' tanks owing to their large glass window cabs. These last two locomotives were taken out of service in 1948. **p. 424**

67097/9, 67100

Class F1. Parker's 5'7" 2–4–2T's for the M.S. & L.R., they were initially fitted with round-topped boilers, but these were later changed to Belpaire fireboxes in conformity with class F2. Originally a class of 39 engines, built 1889–92, they were all scrapped by 1949. **p. 424**

67104–9, 67111–3

Class F2, Pollitt version of class F1, with Belpaire fireboxes. Ten engines built in 1896 and the last survivor withdrawn in 1950. **p. 424**

67114/5/7/9, 67124/6–8, 67134/9–41/3/9, 67150

Class F3. J. Holden's 5'8" 2–4–2T's, originally 50 engines, built 1893–1902. The last of the class, No. 67127, was withdrawn in 1953. **p. 425**

67151–67187

Class F4. Worsdell 5'4" 2–4–2T's for the G.E.R. The class originally consisted of 160 locomotives constructed between 1884 and 1909. Scrapping commenced in 1913, but 30 were rebuilt as class F5 and two others as class F6. No. 67157 was the last survivor and this was scrapped in 1956. **p. 425**

67188–67217

Class F5; the 30 engines mentioned in the last entry, all rebuilt from class F4, and all withdrawn by 1958. **p. 426**

67218–67239

Class F6, the final series of G.E.R. 2–4–2T's, built 1911–12 with 5'4" wheels and larger side tanks. All originally had the later style of lipped chimney, but one or two later acquired the stove pipe pattern as shown in the illustration of No. 67193 (see page 426). Nos. 67218/9, rebuilt from class F4, retained the smaller side tanks. All scrapped by 1958. **p. 427**

67240–67349

Class G5. N.E.R. Worsdell 5'1" 0–4–4T's, 110 engines built 1894–1901. 30 of the class were taken out of service between 1948 and 1954, and the remainder had all gone by 1958. **pp. 427–8**

67350–67395, 67397–9

Class C12. G.N.R. Ivatt 5'8" 4–4–2T's consisting of 60 engines built between 1898 and 1907, mostly for London suburban services, being fitted with condensing apparatus for working through the Metropolitan tunnels. On being replaced by the larger N2 0–6–2T's, this apparatus was removed and the class drafted to work country branches. Ten of the class were scrapped prior to the war and consequently were not included in the 1946 renumbering scheme. Most of the remainder lasted well into the 1950s, but all had disappeared by 1958. **p. 429**

67400–67439

Class C13. G.C.R. Robinson 5'7" 4–4–2T's, built 1903–5 and later superheated. All were in service until 1952 but most of them went during the years 1955–9, and the last one, No. 67417, at the beginning of 1960. **p. 430**

67440–67451

Class C14, an enlarged version of class C13, consisting of 12 locomotives built in 1907 and later fitted with superheaters. Practically all were scrapped in 1957 and the last in service, No. 67450, was withdrawn in 1960. **p. 430**

67452–67481

Class C15, N.B.R. Reid 5'9" 4–4–2T's, a class of 30 engines, built 1911–13. Scrapping began in 1952; all had gone by 1956, except Nos. 67460 and 67474, which were motor-fitted and lasted until 1960. **p. 431**

67482–67502

Class C16, a superheated version of class C15 (above). There were 21 engines built between 1915 and 1921, of which two were withdrawn in 1955. All had gone by 1961. - **p. 431**

67600–67691

Class V1 & V3. Gresley 5'8" 3-cylinder 2–6–2T's, 92 engines built 1932–9. The last ten were built with higher boiler pressure and classified V3, but were identical in appearance with the later locomotives of class V1. Certain engines of class V1 were rebuilt as class V3. Withdrawal commenced in 1960, and all had gone by 1964. **p. 432**

67701–67800

Class L1, 100 engines built 1946–50, 2-cylinder 2–6–4T's with 5'2" wheels. The first four were constructed in 1946 and at the close of 1947 as L.N.E.R. Nos. 9000–9003, followed at the beginning of 1948 by British Railways Nos. E9004–E9012 and 69013–69015. To avoid confusion with other classes, Nos. 69050, etc., it was then decided to renumber the class into the 67700 series, but oddly enough they became Nos. 67701–67716 instead of Nos. 67700–67715. The remainder were now built as Nos. 67717–67800. Withdrawn 1960-2. **p. 433**

68006–68080

Class J94. War Department type of 0–6–0ST, several hundreds of which were built between 1943 and 1945. 75 were purchased by the L.N.E.R. in 1945 and numbered 8006–8080. Withdrawal commenced in 1960. The last two, Nos. 68006 and 68012, were withdrawn in 1967 on closure of the Cromford & High Peak Railway. No. 68077 has been preserved, as have many others of the class built for the War Department which never came into B.R.'s hands. **p. 433**

68081

Class Y5, G.E.R. 3'7" 0–4–0ST, one of a class of four locomotives built 1874–1903. The other three were withdrawn 1926–31, but No. 7230, the 1903 engine, was retained for Departmental duties at Stratford works and finally scrapped in 1948. **p. 434**

68082/3

Class Y6, G.E.R. 0–4–0T tram engines with 3'1" wheels and inside cylinders. Six in class, built 1883–97 for the Wisbech and Upwell Tramway. No. 68082 was withdrawn in 1951 and No. 68083 in 1952. **p. 434**

68088/9

Class Y7. N.E.R. Worsdell 3'5" 0–4–0T's, initially a class of 24 engines built between 1888 and 1923. Of the two surviving locomotives, 68088 finished up on

Departmental duties at Stratford (finally allocated Service No. D34 but not carried), while No. 68089 worked the last passenger trains on the North Sunderland Railway. Both were sold in 1952, the second to a firm of contractors for constructional work on Morecambe promenade. No. 68088 has been preserved.

p. 435

68090/1

Class Y8, being a smaller version of class Y7, constructed for the North Eastern by Worsdell with marine type boiler. No. 8090 was scrapped in 1948, and the second locomotive became shed pilot at York, renumbered D55, but was withdrawn in 1956.

p. 435

68092–68124

Class Y9. North British 3'8" 0–4–0ST's, originally a class of 38 engines built 1882–99. 33 were still running in 1948 and, of these, ten were still in service at the beginning of 1960. All withdrawn by 1963, but No. 68095 has been preserved.

p. 436

68125–68129

Class Y4. G.E.R. Hill 0–4–0T's, a class of five engines built between 1913 and 1920. No. 68129 became D33 in 1952 and was in service until 1962. The others were scrapped between 1955 and 1957.

p. 437

68130–68153 (Class Y1), 68154–68169, 68171–68185 (Class Y3)

L.N.E.R. 4-wheeled Sentinel shunting locomotives, with 2'6" wheels, vertical water tube-boiler, and Poppet valves. Class Y3 had a two-speed gear-box, whereas class Y1 had only a single speed, but the classes were identical in appearance. Nos. 68130–3/6, 68165/6/8, 68173/7/8 and 68181 were renumbered into the Departmental list in 1953 as Nos. D 37, 39, 4, 6, 51, 5, 7, 38, 40, 41, 42 and 3 respectively. In 1955 No. 68183 became No. D8 and in 1956 Nos. 68162 and 68160 became Nos. D21 and D57. The last three survivors were withdrawn in 1964, but No. 68153 has been preserved.

p. 437

68186, 68187

Class Y10. L.N.E.R. double-ended super-Sentinel locomotives with 3'2" wheels, a class of two engines built in 1930. They were at first used on the Wisbech and Upwell Tramway and later on the Yarmouth quayside lines. No. 8187 was taken out of service in 1948 and the other engine in 1952.

p. 438

99

68190/1 (Class Z4), **68192/3** (Class Z5)

Great North of Scotland 0–4–2T's, four engines built in 1915 for shunting duties at Aberdeen Harbour. Class Z4 locomotives had 3'6" wheels, while the somewhat larger Z5's had 4'0" wheels. All scrapped between 1956 and 1960.

p. 438

68200/1/3

Class J62. Great Central Pollitt 3'6" 0–6–0ST's, a class of 12 engines built in 1897. The three surviving locomotives were taken out of service between 1949 and 1951. **p. 439**

68204–68210

Class J63. G.C.R. 3'6" 0–6–0T's, a side tank version of class J62, comprising seven locomotives built between 1906 and 1914 for shunting in Immingham docks. All scrapped by 1957. **p. 439**

68211/3–5

Class J65, G.E.R. Holden 4'0" 0–6–0T's, a class of 20 engines, built 1888–93. The last survivor of the class was scrapped in 1956. **p. 440**

68216–68226

Class J70. G.E.R. 0–6–0T outside-cylinder tram engines with 3'1" wheels. 12 in class, built 1903–21 for the Wisbech and Upwell Tramway and for Yarmouth and Ipswich quayside duties. One engine scrapped in 1942 and the others between 1949 and 1955. **p. 440**

68230–6/8–40/2–56/8–60, 68262–73, 68275–68314/6

Class J71. N.E.R. Worsdell 0–6–0T's with 4'7" wheels, a class of originally 120 engines built 1886–95. All scrapped by 1961. **p. 441**

68317/9

Class J55, survivors of Stirling's earlier G.N.R. 4'8" 0–6–0ST's, of which 105 were built from 1874 to 1891, originally with domeless boilers. These last two of the class were scrapped in 1948 and 1950. **p. 441**

68320–68354

Class J88. North British Reid 3'9" dock tank, with outside cylinders, was built between 1905 and 1919. The class as a whole was scrapped between the years 1954 and 1962. **p. 442–3**

68355–68364

Class J73. Worsdell 4'7" 0–6–0T's for the North Eastern. Ten engines built 1891–2, all of which were withdrawn between 1955 and 1960. **p. 443**

68365

Class J75, last survivor of a class of 16 Hull and Barnsley 0–6–0T's, built 1901–8, originally with domeless boilers. This locomotive was withdrawn from service in 1949 as No. 8365 without receiving its British Railways' number.

p. 444

68366/8

Class J60. Two survivors of four 0–6–0T's, built in 1897 for the Lancashire, Derbyshire and East Coast Railway (absorbed by the Great Central in 1907) and scrapped in 1948. **p. 444**

68370–68388

Class J66. 50 4'0" 0–6–0T's built by Holden from 1886–8 for the Great Eastern. All were withdrawn by 1954, except Nos. 68370/8, 68382/3, the first three of which were renumbered in 1953 into the Departmental stock as Nos. D32, 36 and 31 respectively. No. 68383 was withdrawn in 1955, and D31 and D36 in 1959, leaving only D32 early in 1960. This locomotive was withdrawn in 1962.

p. 445

68390–3, 68395–68402, 68404–10/2/7, 68420–68438, 68440/1

Class J77. Originally Fletcher 0–4–4 well tanks for the N.E.R., built 1874–84, and rebuilt at York and Darlington as 4'1" 0–6–0T's between 1907 and 1921. In all 60 locomotives were converted. The last of these engines was taken out of service in 1961. **pp. 445–6**

68442–68461, 68463–68481

Class J83. N.B.R. Holmes 4'6" 0–6–0T's, comprising 40 engines built from 1900 to 1901. No. 8462 was scrapped in 1947 and others followed from 1956 onwards, leaving only about 15 of them still running in 1961, the last going in 1962. **p. 446**

101

68484/8/9

Class J93, survivors of a set of nine 0–6–0T's acquired by the L.N.E.R. from the Midland and Great Northern Joint Railway in 1937. Some were built new at Melton Constable between 1897 and 1905, while others were partly rebuilds of Cornwall Mineral Railway engines built 1873–4. The last survivor of the class, No. 8489, was taken out of service in 1949. None received its allocated British Railways' number before being scrapped. **p. 447**

68490–68505, 68507–68538, 68540–68563, 68565–68579, 68581, 68583–68603, 68605–68613, 68616–9, 68621/3/5/6/8/9, 68630–3/5/6

Classes J67 and J69. G.E.R. Holden 4′0″ 0–6–0T's, originally a class of 160 engines, built 1886–1904. There were many minor variations in this series and many of the locomotives were rebuilt between the two classes, in some instances more than once. The main difference in external appearance between classes J67 and J69 lay in the larger tanks of the latter class. No. 68532 was transferred to Departmental stock as D43 in 1959, but scrapped later in that year; during the same year Nos. 68498 and 68543 became D44 and D45. Withdrawals were heavy from 1958 onwards, and the last of them went in 1962. No. 68633 has been preserved as G.E.R. No. 87. **pp. 447–8**

68638–68666

Class J68, the last class of G.E.R. 0–6–0T's, built 1912–23, with larger tanks (similar to those of class J69) and side window cabs. One engine was sold to the War Department in 1940 and many were scrapped from 1958 onwards, the last in 1962. **p. 449**

68667–68669

Class J92. G.E.R. 0–6–0T Crane engines for use at Stratford works. Originally built in 1868, they were reconstructed between 1891 and 1894 when the cranes were added. After rebuilding they were known on the G.E.R. and L.N.E.R. until 1946 simply as 'B', 'C', and 'D'. They were scrapped between 1950 and 1952. **p. 449**

68670–68754, 69001–69028

Class J72, a unique class of Worsdell 0–6–0T's. The original 85 engines were built between 1898 and 1925, the class being perpetuated by British Railways and a further 28 locomotives constructed 1949–51. No parallel example can be found in the British Isles, and probably not in the world, of a design being constructed at intervals over a period of fifty-four years practically without alteration. Scrapping of the earlier engines commenced in 1958, but about half of these

102

and all the later ones were still running in 1961. By the end of 1963 all the original engines had gone, the last survivors being Nos. 68723 and 68736, which had been repainted in N.E.R. colours for station pilot work at Newcastle, and there were only four survivors of the post-Nationalisation batch in service, these too being withdrawn in 1964. No. 69023 has been preserved, painted in N.E.R. colours, and carries the name *Joem*. **p. 450**

68757–68781, 68783–68889

Class J52 Stirling and Ivatt 4′8″ 0–6–0ST's constructed for the Great Northern. Built between 1892 and 1909, there were originally 137 locomotives in the class. The earlier engines had domeless boilers as first built, some being fitted with condensing apparatus for working through the Metropolitan tunnels. Nos. 68845 and 68816 were renumbered 1 and 2 in the Departmental stock. Withdrawals were heavy after 1954 and the last survivor went in 1961. No. 68846 has been preserved, restored to its G.N.R. livery as No. 1247. **p. 451**

68890–68991

Class J50. Great Northern Gresley 0–6–0T's with 4′8″ wheels. The class consisted of 102 engines built 1913–1937. Withdrawal commenced in 1959 and by 1963 only seven remained, these having been all renumbered into the Departmental list as Nos. 10–16 (formerly Nos. 68911, 68914, 68917, 68928, 68961, 68971 and 68976). **p. 452**

69050–69062, 69064–9

Class L3. G.C.R. Robinson 5′1″ 2–6–4T's for freight work. A class of 20 engines built 1914–17 and all withdrawn from 1947 to 1955. **p. 453**

69070/1

Class L2, the surviving locomotives of a class of six Metropolitan 2–6–4T's, with 5′6″ driving wheels, acquired by the L.N.E.R. from the London Passenger Transport Board in 1937. Constructed in 1924 from parts of S.E. & C.R. class N 2–6–0's; partly built at Woolwich in 1919 but not completed. Both were scrapped in 1948. **p. 454**

69076/7

Class M2, being the surviving locomotives of four Metropolitan 5′9″ 0–6–4T's, taken over by the L.N.E.R. in 1937 from the L.P.T.B. Originally built in 1915, both were taken out of service in 1948. **p. 454**

103

69089

Class N12, the last locomotive of a set of nine Hull and Barnsley 4'6" 0–6–2T's. Built in 1901, originally with a domeless boiler, this engine was scrapped in 1948. **p. 455**

69090–69109

Class N10. North Eastern Worsdell 4'7" 0–6–2T's built between 1902–3. No. 9103 was scrapped in 1948, but three of them lasted until 1962. **p. 455**

69110–69119

Class N13. Hull and Barnsley 4'6" 0–6–2T's, an enlarged version of class N12, built 1913–14. The last surviving engine, No. 69114, was scrapped in 1956.

p. 456

69120/4/5

Class N14. N.B.R. Reid 4'6" 0–6–2T's, built in 1909. Designed for banking on the Cowlairs incline, there were six engines in the class, all of which were withdrawn by 1954. **p. 456**

69126–69224

Class N15, a development of class N14 (above), comprising 99 locomotives built between 1910 and 1924. The first six of the class, Nos. 69126–69131, were intended for work on the Cowlairs incline and had the larger bunkers as fitted to class N14. Scrapping began in 1957, and by 1961 only about 30 remained. They all went in 1962. **p. 457**

69225–69237, 69239–69247

Class N4. Parker 5'1" 0–6–2T's for the Manchester, Sheffield and Lincolnshire Railway, originally 55 engines constructed 1889–92, with round-topped boilers, but subsequently converted to Belpaire. The last of the class to remain in service were scrapped at the close of 1954. **p. 458**

69250–69370

Class N5. M.S. & L.R. 5'1" 0–6–2T's, a class of 129 engines built between 1891 and 1901. No. 69250 was the first locomotive in this country to be fitted with a Belpaire firebox. No. 69270 and one other (taken out of service in 1936 and con-

104

sequently not included in the renumbering scheme) were built new for the Wrexham, Mold and Connah's Quay Railway to the G.C.R. design. This line was absorbed by the Great Central in 1905. Withdrawals were heavy after 1954, and the last survivor was condemned in 1961.   **p. 458**

69371–69387, 69389–69401 (Class N8), 69410/1/3–5, 69418–69429 Class N9)

Class N8 consisted originally of 62 engines, 5'1" 0–6–2T's, built by T. W. Worsdell in 1886–90 for the North Eastern. As first constructed, they were Worsdell-von Borries 2-cylinder compounds, but were later all converted to 'simples' and some fitted with superheaters and/or piston valves. Class N8 was extinct by 1956. Class N9 was 20 somewhat similar engines built new as 'simples' in 1893–4 by Wilson Worsdell, and all scrapped by 1955.   **p. 459**

69430–7, 69439–69485

Class N1. Great Northern Ivatt 0–6–2T's, with 5'8" wheels, built between 1906 and 1912. A class of 56 engines, of which No. 9438 was withdrawn in 1947. Most of the class were originally fitted with condensing apparatus for working through the Metropolitan tunnels, but many later worked in the Leeds and Bradford districts and with some of these locomotives the apparatus was removed. A few engines in this class received superheaters. The majority of the class were still running in 1954, but all had been taken out of service by 1959, although No. 69461 was still in use until 1962 as a stationary boiler at Shoeburyness for the purposes of warming coaching stock.   **pp. 460–1**

69490–69596

Class N2, Gresley's development of class N1, with larger boilers, superheaters and piston valves. Some were fitted with condensing apparatus and shorter chimneys for working on the Metropolitan widened lines. A few were transferred to the Glasgow area. All of the class was withdrawn between 1959 and 1962. No. 69523 has been preserved, restored as L.N.E.R. 4744.   **pp. 461–2**

69600–69621

Class N7/4. Hill's design of 4'10" 0–6–2T's for the Great Eastern suburban services. Built between 1915 and 1924, originally with Belpaire fireboxes, but all eventually received Gresley round-topped boilers. Scrapping began in 1958 and all had gone by 1962, but No. 69621 has been retained for preservation.   **p. 462**

69622–69733

Classes N7/1, N7/2, N7/3 and N7/5, Gresley's development of the original G.E.R. design, some constructed with Belpaire fireboxes, but most of the later ones were built new with round-topped boilers. The majority of the Belpaires were subsequently rebuilt to conform with the later locomotives. All were taken out of service 1958–62. **p. 463**

69800–69829

Class A5/1. Great Central Robinson 5'7" 4–6–2T's, originally 31 engines built 1911–23. One locomotive, not included in the renumbering scheme, was scrapped in 1942, but the remainder were still in service in 1957. All of these locomotives had gone, however, by 1961. **p. 464**

69830–69842

Class A5/2, 13 engines similar to class A5/1, but with differences in detail. Built by Gresley in 1925–6 for use in the North Eastern area around Middlesbrough. All scrapped in 1957–8. **p. 464**

69791–69799

Class A6. North Eastern 5'7" 4–6–2T's, a class of ten locomotives constructed in 1907–8, originally as 4–6–0T's, but later rebuilt as 4–6–2T's. They were known as the 'Whitby Tanks' as they were built for the steeply graded Whitby-Scarborough line. No. 9790 was broken up in 1947, while the remaining nine went between 1948 and 1953. **p. 465**

69770–69789

Class A7. Raven 3-cylinder 4'7" freight 4–6–2T's for the North Eastern, built 1910–11. All scrapped by 1957. **p. 466**

69850–69894

Class A8. N.E.R. 5'9" 3-cylinder 4–6–2T's, initially built 1913–21 as 4–4–4T's. They were converted to 4–6–2T type between 1931 and 1936. All of these were scrapped between 1957 and 1960. **p. 466**

69900–69903

Class S1/1. Robinson heavy 3-cylinder 4'8" 0–8–4T's, built in 1908 for shunting in Wath marshalling yard. No. 69901 was rebuilt in 1932 with a booster to the rear bogie, the booster being later removed. This locomotive was classified S1/2. All scrapped by 1957. **p. 467**

69904/5

Class S1/3, being Gresley's development of the original Great Central design, built in 1932 with booster, which was later removed. Both scrapped by 1957.

p. 467

69910–69922

Class T1. North Eastern 3-cylinder 4′7″ 4–8–0T's, designed for heavy shunting duties. Ten engines were built in 1909 and a further five in 1925. Two of the original lot were scrapped in 1937, but the remainder were all still in service until 1955, two more being withdrawn in that year and others since. The last survivor, No. 69921, was scrapped in 1961.

p. 468

69925–69937

Class Q1, 13 Great Central 0–8–0's of class Q4 (see 63200, etc., page 90) rebuilt by Thompson as 0–8–0T's for heavy shunting. All scrapped between 1954 and 1959.

p. 468

69999

Class U1. Gresley 2 8 8 2T Garratt, built 1925 for banking on the Worsborough incline. In anticipation of its becoming redundant because of the electrification of the Wath-Penistone line (completed 1953), it was given trials in 1949 on the Lickey incline. The year 1955 saw its conversion to an oil burner, but it was finally withdrawn from traffic at the end of that year without being put into regular traffic.

p. 469

2136

Sentinel Rail Car, *Hope*, last survivor of a series of 50 gear-driven rail cars built by the Sentinel Company between 1928 and 1931, with 3′1″ wheels. All were withdrawn between 1943 and 1948. It is interesting to note that this class was named after famous stage coaches.

p. 469

BRITISH RAILWAYS' STANDARD DESIGNS

Class List - Historical Data
List of Illustrations

70000–70054

'Britannia' class 'Pacifics', the first British Railways' standard design introduced in 1951, with 6'2" driving wheels and 2 outside cylinders. The last ten to be constructed, Nos. 70045–70054, were turned out in 1954. Many of the class were named after poets, but Nos. 70014–70029 perpetuated the names of famous Great Western locomotives of the past. Nos. 70050–70054, originally allocated to Scotland, were named after Scottish firths. The last survivor, No. 70013, *Oliver Cromwell*, withdrawn in 1968, has been preserved, along with the original 70000 *Britannia*.   **p. 473**

71000

Duke of Gloucester, 3 cylinders, 6'2" driving wheels, and fitted with Caprotti valve gear. Built in 1954 as the prototype of a new standard design for top-link main line duties, it was unfortunately destined to remain the sole representative of its class, through the abandonment of the new construction of steam locomotives. Withdrawn in 1962.   **p. 474**

72000–72009

A 'Pacific' design of somewhat lighter construction than the 'Britannia' class, with 6'2" wheels and 2 outside cylinders. Ten engines, named after Scottish clans, were built in 1952 and were allocated to Scotland. A further fifteen were on order, five for the Southern and another ten for Scotland, but these were never built. Withdrawn 1962–6.   **p. 474**

73000–73171

Standard class 5 mixed traffic 4–6–0's, based largely on the similar L.M.S. design introduced by Sir William Stanier in 1934. The British Railways' version first appeared in 1951 and construction proceeded until 1957. Nos. 73125–73154 had Caprotti valve gear. All withdrawn 1964–8. Nos. 73050 and 73129 have been preserved. **p. 475**

75000–75079

Class 4 4–6–0's for light passenger and general duties. They had 5'8" driving wheels and 2 outside cylinders. Introduced in 1951, construction proceeded until 1957. A few were fitted with a double blastpipe and chimney. All withdrawn 1964–8. Nos. 75027, 75029, 75069 and 75078 have been preserved, with the possibility of others. **p. 476**

76000–76114

Class 4 2–6–0's, with 5'3" driving wheels. They were of slightly smaller capacity than the 75000 class 4–6–0's. The class was introduced in 1953 and construction continued until 1957. 5'3" driving wheels, with 2 outside cylinders. Withdrawn 1964–7. Nos. 76017 and 76077 still in existence at Barry in 1973, with possibility of preservation. **p. 476**

77000–77019

Class 3 2–6–0's, with 5'3" driving wheels and 2 outside cylinders. This class consisted of 20 engines only, built in 1954. An order for a further five of this class was cancelled. Withdrawn 1965–7. **p. 477**

78000–78064

Light 2–6–0's, class 2, with 5'0" driving wheels and 2 outside cylinders. The class was similar in almost all respects to Ivatt's L.M.S. design introduced in 1946. The British Railways' locomotives were constructed from 1953 to 1956. All withdrawn 1963–7. Nos. 78018, 78019, 78022 and 78059 still in existence at Barry in 1973, offering possibilities of preservation. **p. 477**

80000–80154

Standard 2–6–4T's, class 4, passenger tank based on the numerous class built for the L.M.S. by Stanier and Fairburn, originating from Sir Henry Fowler's design of 1927. The class had 5'8" wheels and 2 outside cylinders. They were built from 1951 onwards and construction continued until 1957. No. 80103 went in 1962, and general withdrawal commenced in 1964, being completed by 1967. Nos. 80002 and 80079 have been preserved. Several still in existence at Barry in 1973, amongst which No. 80064, 80105 and 80151 have been earmarked for preservation. **p. 478**

82000–82044

Class 3 2–6–2T's for passenger work, with 5'3" driving wheels and 2 outside cylinders. Built between 1952 and 1955. All withdrawn 1964–7.   **p. 478**

84000–84029

Class 2 light 2–6–2T's, for light passenger working, Nos. 84000–84019 being motor-fitted for pull-and-push trains. Generally similar in design to Ivatt's L.M.S. design of 1946 but with 5'0" wheels and 2 outside cylinders. Nos. 84000–84019 were built in 1953 and 84020–84029 in 1957. All withdrawn 1963–5.

p. 479

90000–90732

War-time Austerity 2–8–0's designed by Riddles and constructed in large numbers from 1943 onwards. 4'8½" driving wheels with 2 outside cylinders. 200 of these locomotives were purchased by the L.N.E.R. in 1947, and these, together with 533 others which had been on loan to pre-Nationalisation companies, eventually became British Railways' stock and were renumbered into one series as Nos. 90000–90732. All were scrapped between 1959 and 1967. It is a little surprising that none of this very numerous class survived for preservation.

p. 479

90750–90774

War-time Austerity 2–10–0's, designed by Riddles and built from 1943 onwards, with 4'8½" wheels and 2 outside cylinders. 25 of these locomotives were absorbed into British Railways' stock in 1948 as Nos. 90750–90774. All were scrapped in the years 1961–2.   **p. 480**

92000–92250

British Railways' standard 2–10–0 freight locomotives, with 5'0" driving wheels and 2 outside cylinders. They were built from 1954 onwards and construction was not completed until early in 1960. Nos. 92020–92029 were constructed with Franco-Crosti boilers, but these were later removed. No. 92250 was fitted experimentally in 1959 with a Giesl ejector, involving a modified type of chimney. No. 92220, turned out at Swindon in March 1960, was the last steam locomotive to be built for British Railways. It was specially painted in G.W.R. green, provided with a copper-capped chimney and appropriately named *Evening Star*. Withdrawal commenced in 1964, but a few survived in service until the end of steam in 1968. Nos. 92203 and 92220 have been preserved. A few others remained at Barry in 1973, amongst which No. 92212 is a possible candidate for preservation.   **pp. 480–2**

Illustrations

THE GREAT WESTERN GROUP

No. 1 *Hercules*, acquired from the Ystalyfera Tin Works.

Corris Railway No. 3 after the closing of the line and before being acquired by the Tal-y-Llyn Railway.

117

Corris Railway No. 4, as running on the Tal-y-Llyn Railway.

No. 5 *Portishead*, acquired in 1940 from the Weston, Clevedon & Portishead Railway. Originally a Stroudley 'Terrier' from the L.B. & S.C.R.

Vale of Rheidol narrow-gauge 2–6–2T No. 8 *Llywelyn.*

Former Cleobury, Mortimer & Ditton Priors Light Railway 0–6–0PT No. 28.

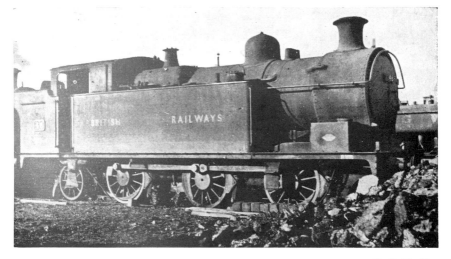

R. J. Buckley

Rhymney Railway class R 0–6–2T No. 46.

W. Potter

Rhymney Railway class M 0–6–2T No. 47, rebuilt with Great Western boiler.

Rhymney Railway class R1 0–6–2T No. 37, with old-type boiler.

Rhymney Railway class R1 0–6–2T No. 40, as rebuilt with G.W.R. boiler.

Rhymney Railway class A 0–6–2T No. 67, with earlier type of boiler.

Rhymney Railway class A 0–6–2T No. 66, rebuilt with Great Western boiler.

Rhymney Railway class P 0–6–2T No. 83, with G.W.R. boiler.

Rhymney Railway class S1 0–6–0T No. 92.

Rhymney Railway class S 0–6–0T No. 95, with original cab.

Rhymney Railway class S 0–6–0T No. 96, with modified cab.

124

Cardiff Railway 0–6–2T No. 155.

W. Potter

Port Talbot Railway 0–6–2T No. 184.

W. Potter

Alexandra Docks 0–6–2ST No. 190.

Taff Vale Railway 0-6-OT Nos. 193, 194 and 195.

Barry Railway 0–6–2T No. 272.

Llanelly & Mynydd Mawr 0–6–0ST No. 359 *Hilda*.

Taff Vale Railway O4 class 0–6–2T No. 302, allocated new number 202, but scrapped in 1948 without actually carrying it.

Taff Vale Railway O4 class 0-6-2T No. 297 as rebuilt with Great Western boiler and modified side tank.

Taff Vale Railway A class 0–6–2T No. 344, with original round-topped side tanks.

Taff Vale Railway A class 0–6–2T No. 309, with modified side tanks.

W. Potter

Taff Vale Railway O3 class 0–6–2T No. 410.

Brecon & Merthyr Railway 5′0″ 0–6–2T No. 434, rebuilt with G.W.R. boiler. Some still retained the old-type boiler, as in the illustration of No. 425 (page 131) of the 4′6″ class.

F. Jones

Brecon & Merthyr Railway 4′6″ 0–6–2T No. 425, with old boiler.

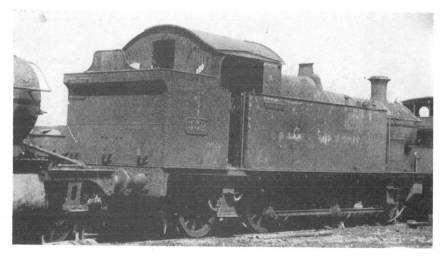

Brecon & Merthyr Railway 4′6″ 0–6–2T No. 332 (allocated No. 423 but scrapped in 1950 without being renumbered), rebuilt with Great Western boiler and modified cab.

Alexandra Docks 0–6–0T No. 666.

Alexandra Docks 0–6–0ST No. 680.

Cardiff Railway 0–6–0PT No. 682.

Llanelly & Mynydd Mawr Railway 0–6–0T No. 803.

W. Potter

Barry Railway 0–6–0T No. 784 with old boiler.

W. Potter

Barry Railway 0–6–0T No. 783, rebuilt with extended smokebox and modified **bunker.**

R. M. Casserley

Welshpool & Llanfair Railway narrow gauge 0–6–0T No. 822 *The Earl.*

R. M. Casserley

Cambrian Railway 0–6–0 No. 849.

Hawksworth 4-6-0 No. 1019 *County of Merioneth.*

K. Leech

No. 1000 *County of Middlesex* with double chimney.

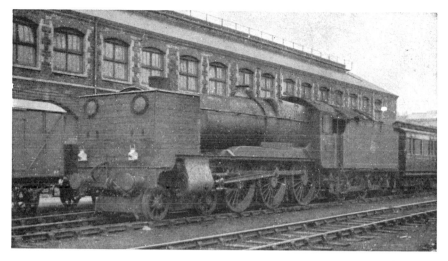

W. Potter

No. 1009 *County of Carmarthen*, as running experimentally in 1954 with stove-pipe chimney and indicator shelter.

1101–1106

G.W.R. 0–4–0T

Avonside 0-4-0T dock shunter No. 1105.

Swansea Harbour Trust, Barclay 0–4–0ST No. 1140.

Swansea Harbour Trust, Peckett 0–4–0ST No. 1141.

Swansea Harbour Trust, Hudswell Clarke 0–4–0ST No. 1142.

Swansea Harbour Trust, Peckett 0–4–0ST No. 968, later renumbered 1143.

Swansea Harbour Trust, Hawthorn Leslie 0–4–0ST No. 1144.

Swansea Harbour Trust, Peckett 0–4–0ST No. 1098, later renumbered 1145.

Swansea Harbour Trust, Peckett 0–6–0ST No. 1085, later renumbered 1146.

Powlesland & Mason, Peckett 0–4–0ST No. 779, later renumbered 1151.

Powlesland & Mason, Hawthorn Leslie 0–4–0ST No. 942, later renumbered 1153.

Cambrian Railway 2–4–0T No. 1196.

R. M. Casserley

Alexandra Docks 2-6-2T No. 1205.

Liskeard & Looe Railway 2-4-0T No. 1308 *Lady Margaret*. This engine later carried a considerably shorter chimney.

143

Whitland & Cardigan Railway 0–6–0ST No. 1331.

R. M. Casserley

Midland & South Western Junction Railway 2–4–0 No. 1335.

R. M. Casserley

Cardiff Railway 0–4–0ST No. 1338.

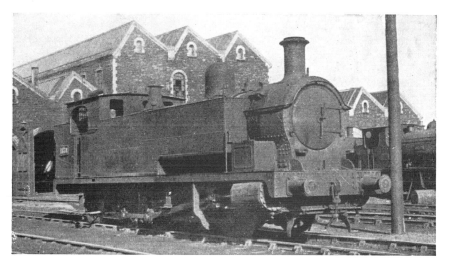

Port Talbot Railway 0–8–2T No. 1358.

Churchward 0–6–0ST No. 1365, specially designed for dock shunting.

R. M. Casserley

Collett 0-6-0PT No. 1367 at Weymouth with Channel Islands boat train.

146

R. M. Casserley

Collett motor fitted 0-4-2T No. 1465.

R. M. Casserley

0-4-2T No. 1420, fitted with top feed, at Radley with the Abingdon branch train, a typical G.W.R. pull-and-push unit.

Hawksworth heavy 0-6-0PT with outside cylinders and Walschaert valve gear.

Hawksworth light 0–6–0PT No. 1644.

Earlier Swindon and Wolverhampton design of 4'7½" 0-6-0PT No. 2718 with open cab.

4'7½" 0-6-0PT No. 2779 with all-over cab.

149

Earlier Swindon and Wolverhampton design of 4'1½" 0–6–0PT. No. 1925, one of the two engines still carrying the old type of round saddle tank in 1948, all the other existing locomotives of the class having acquired the square pannier tanks.

No. 1965. The four illustrations on these two pages depict varying types of cabs and bunkers found in this class.

No. 2089 fitted with bell for street and dock working at Birkenhead.

No. 2156 with all-over cab, after overhaul at Derby in 1950.

R. M. Casserley

Burry Port & Gwendraeth Valley Railway 0–6–0T No. 2166, with old-type boiler and safety valves.

No. 2167, rebuilt with boiler carrying Great Western fittings.

W. Potter

Burry Port & Gwendraeth Valley Railway 0–6–0ST No. 2176.

W. Potter

Burry Port & Gwendraeth Valley Railway No. 2193 *Burry Port*.

Burry Port & Gwendraeth Valley Railway No. 2195 *Cwm Mawr*. The name plate was later removed.

Burry Port & Gwendraeth Valley Railway 0–6–0ST No. 2196 *Gwendraeth*.

W. Potter

Burry Port & Gwendraeth Valley Railway 0–6–0T No. 2197 *Pioneer*.

Between 2612 and 2680   2–6–0 Aberdare

Dean outside framed 2–6–0 No. 2620.

R. M. Casserley

Dean 0–6–0 No. 2538, final survivor of a famous class, on one of its last passenger duties at Three Cocks Junction in September, 1956.

Dean 0-6-0 No. 2356 with top-feed apparatus.

Collett 0–6–0 No. 3201 with large R.O.D. tender. Most of the class are in opera-
tion with the smaller Churchward or Collett tenders.

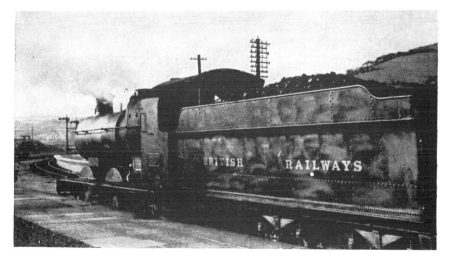

No. 2223, without side windows to cab. Nos. 2211–2240, which were built
during 1940–4, were designed to assist with black-out regulations, but all were
later given side windows.

157

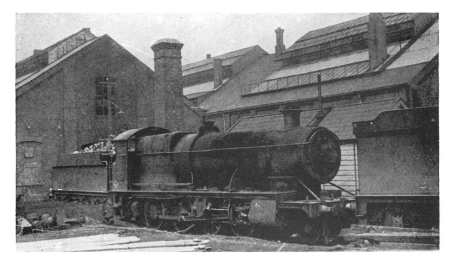

Churchward 2–8–0 No. 2818, with original rectangular front-end framing over cylinders. All later had the modern modified curved front-end framing and outside steam pipes, as in the illustration below.

Collett 2–8–0 No. 3842. These engines differ from the original series in having side window cabs and, on the left-hand side only, combined splashers over the two rear driving wheels.

No. 2839, temporarily renumbered 4804 from 1947 to 1948 when fitted with oil-burning apparatus.

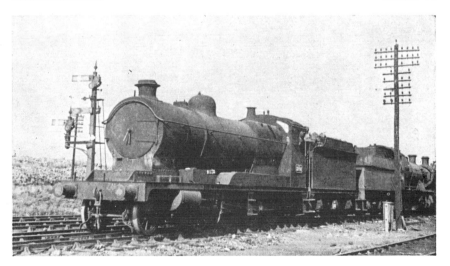

No. 3046, Robinson Great Central-type 2–8–0.

No. 2906 *Lady of Lynn,* one of the earlier engines of this class with raised framing extending to the end of the cab.

No. 2947 *Madresfield Court,* a later engine still running with the inside steam pipes.

No. 2944 *Highnam Court*, as subsequently fitted with outside steam pipes.

No. 2935 *Caynham Court*, with Caprotti valve gear.

161

No. 3170, one of the original Churchward 5'8" 2–6–2T's of 1907, later rebuilt largely in accordance with the subsequent Collett modifications of the class.

No. 8102, one of ten of the original Churchward engines rebuilt by Collett with 5'6" wheels. A further five locomotives were rebuilt with 5'3" wheels and became Nos. 3100–3104. Both of these series had 225 lbs. pressure boilers.

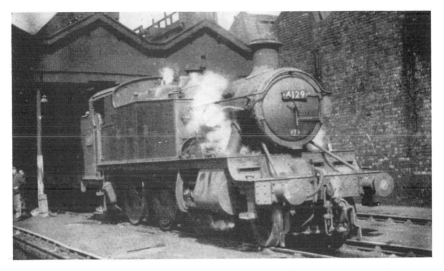

No. 4129, 5100 class 2-6-2T.

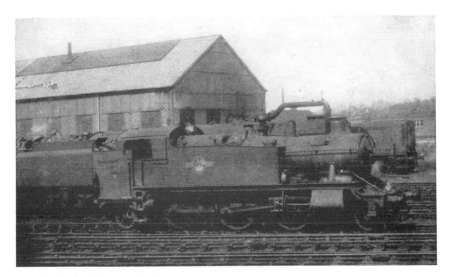

No. 6162, representing the final development of the 5'8" 2-6-2T's with 225 lbs. pressure. Most of the 6100 class were employed on the London suburban services.

R. M. Casserley

No. 3335, the last surviving 'Bulldog' with curved framing.

No. 3341 *Blasius*, one of the earlier straight-framed engines, with combined name and number plate.

No. 3430 *Inchcape*, one of the later series of 'Bulldogs', most of which had the wider chimney as illustrated. Some, however, carried the narrow chimney as in the two illustrations on the opposite page.

3440   Churchward 4–4–0 City

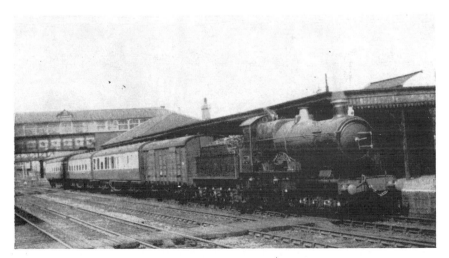

City of Truro was running in ordinary service and working enthusiasts' specials between 1957 and 1962 after spending 26 years in York Museum. It has since found its final resting place in Swindon Museum.

No. 3588, one of the last surviving Dean 2–4–0T's.

Dean 0-4-2T No. 3578. This engine was scrapped in 1945, but was similar to the three which lasted until 1949, Nos. 3574/5/7.

Standard 0–6–0PT No. 8738 in the first style of British Railways' painting, but with Great Western Swindon-type lettering.

No. 8773, showing the modified cab fitted to the later engines of the class.

167

No. 4667, with top-feed apparatus.

No. 5752, one of the earlier series, carrying a spark arrester to the chimney. It is also fitted with top-feed apparatus like No. 4667 above.

No. 6705, one of the non-vacuum-fitted engines. The cabs of this class differ as in the case of the vacuum-fitted locomotives, Nos. 6700–6749 having the earlier cabs and Nos. 6750–6779 the later type.

No. 9705 fitted with condensing apparatus.

No. 4062 *Malmesbury Abbey*, with inside steam pipes with which the class was originally built.

No. 4041 *Prince of Wales*, with 'elbow' pattern outside steam pipes.

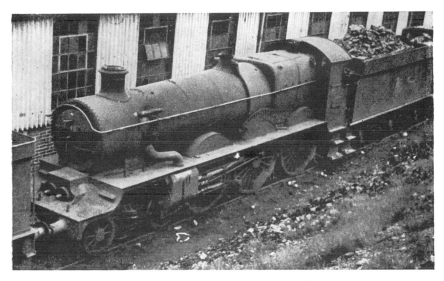

No. 4048 *Princess Victoria*, with standard pattern of outside steam pipes.

No. 111 *Viscount Churchill*, reconstructed from 'Pacific' No. 111 *The Great Bear*.

171

No. 5036 *Lyonshall Castle*, with standard type of G.W.R. tender.

No 7011 *Banbury Castle*, with flat-sided tender and in an early British Railways livery of light brunswick green.

No. 7029 *Clun Castle*, with double chimney.

No. 5086 *Viscount Horne*, with self-weighing tender.

No. 6010 *King Charles I*, with Cornish Riviera Express.

R. J. Buckley

No. 6015 *King Richard III*, fitted with double chimney.

174

No. 5355 with inside steam pipes as originally built. The majority of the class later had outside steam pipes, as in the illustration below.

9300–9319 (now renumbered 7322–7341)   Collett 2–6–0

No. 9319, one of the last twenty which had side-window cabs.

No. 4266, one of the earlier engines with flat framing to the front of the cylinder head. This locomotive is also fitted with inside steam pipes, but the majority later had the outside variety.

No. 4296, with raised framing over cylinder and outside steam pipes.

No. 7225 with framing corresponding to the earlier 2-8-0T's, as illustrated opposite.

No. 7240, with raised type of framing.

No. 4401, with inside steam pipes as originally constructed.

No. 4408, with outside steam pipes.

No. 4510, with inside steam pipes as built.

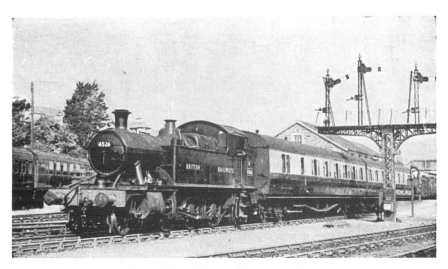

No. 4526, with outside steam pipes.

No. 5563, one of the later Collett engines, similar to the earlier Churchward 4500-4574 series (see previous page), but with sloping side tanks.

No. 4706, one of Churchward's mixed traffic 2-8-0's with 5′8″ wheels.

No. 6660, one of Collett's 0-6-2T's, built principally for work in the South Wales area.

No. 5816. These engines are similar to the 1400 class, but are not motor fitted. Like the 1400's, some of them later had top-feed apparatus.

No. 4900 *Saint Martin*, rebuilt from the 'Saint' class (see pages 160–1) and forming the prototype of the mixed traffic 'Halls'.

No. 6948 *Holbrooke Hall*, one of the earlier standard 'Halls'.

No. 5955 *Garth Hall*, as temporarily renumbered 3950 from 1947 to 1949 while fitted for oil burning.

No. 7918 *Rhose Wood Hall*, one of the later 'Halls', built by Hawksworth with slight modifications.

No. 5407, motor fitted 0–6–0PT with 5'2" wheels. Some of these engines, and also the 6400 and 7400 classes, had top-feed apparatus.

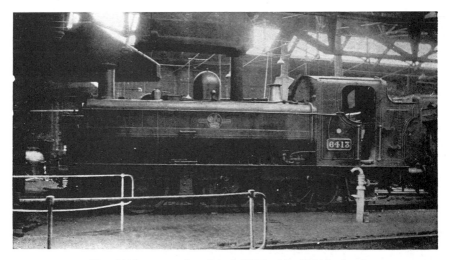

No. 6413, motor fitted 0–6–0PT with 4'7½" wheels.

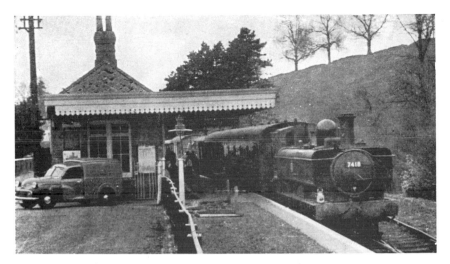

No. 7418, 4′7½″ 0–6–0PT for branch-line work. They are similar to the 6400 class, but not motor fitted. This view was taken at Tetbury.

No. 846), one of the Hawksworth enlarged 1947 design of 0-6-0PT's.

No. 6862 *Derwent Grange*, Collet 5′8″ 4–6–0 for light passenger work.

No. 7808 *Cookham Manor*, with standard wide chimney. A slightly lighter version to the 'Granges' illustrated above.

W. Potter

No. 7818, as running experimentally in 1952.

No. 7824 *Iford Manor*, with modified chimney design.

R. M. Casserley

No. 9054 *Cornubia*, 'Duke of Cornwall' class.

No. 9064, formerly *Trevethick*, 'Duke' class with top-feed apparatus.

R. M. Casserley

No. 9016, 'Earl' class, reconstructed from frames and boilers of withdrawn 'Bulldogs' and 'Dukes'.

No. 9022, 'Earl' class with top-feed apparatus.

189

THE SOUTHERN GROUP

No. 1 (30001). None of the class survived to receive its B.R. allocated number, all being scrapped with the S. R. numbers.

No. 361 (30361), carrying Drummond-type boiler, with pop safety valve on dome. One or two of the class were rebuilt as illustrated, but the great majority remained in practically their original form to the last.

No. 30244 as first repainted British Railways in Southern malachite green.

No. 30132 with leading sandboxes below the running plate, in which form some of the class were originally built.

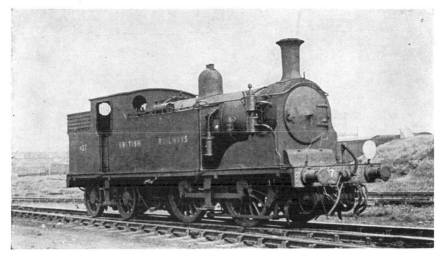

No. S27 (30027), as fitted for pull-and-push working.

No. DS 238 *Wainwright* (late No. 30070), works shunter at Ashford.

No. 89 (30089) *Trouville*, with Adams' boiler. The name was later removed.

No. 30088, with Drummond boiler. One or two of these engines had birdcage spark arresters to the chimney, as in the illustration on page 202.

196

No. 30119, one of the earlier series. For many years this was the locomotive used for working Royal trains on the Southern over lines on which no heavy engine could run. It retained its green livery until scrapped in 1953.

No. 30726, fitted with six-wheeled tender and showing the new type of emblem introduced in 1957.

No. 30301, one of the later series with wider plain splashers, as fitted to engines numbered between 300 and 338.

R. M. Casserley

No. 30338, with the large eight-wheeled tender, with which all of the class were originally fitted.

No. 314 (30314), running as an oil burner. 13 engines of the class were so converted in 1947.

No. 731 (30731), one of the earlier series, as fitted with oil burning apparatus.

No. 341. This locomotive was allocated No. 30341 by British Railways, but was never renumbered.

No. 384, fitted with Urie-type chimney and running with tender formerly belonging to No. 385. Some of these engines were latterly fitted with eight-wheeled tenders, as on the opposite page.

No. 30438. Some of the class had eight-wheeled tenders, as in this illustration, while others were fitted with six-wheeled tenders.

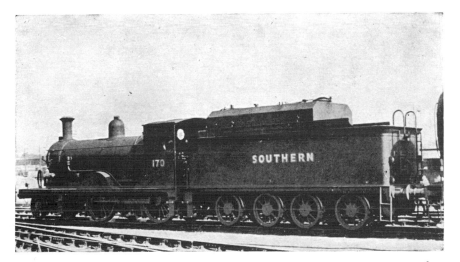

No. 170. This locomotive was allocated No. 30170 by British Railways, but never carried its new number. It was fitted for oil burning in 1947, as were several others of this class.

No. 30213, non-motor fitted.

No. 183 (30183). This illustration shows three different variations to be found in some locomotives of the class. This particular engine embodies a Drummond-type boiler, fitted to some engines of the class, and a birdcage spark-arrester to the chimney; it is also adapted for motor working.

No. W32, *Bonchurch*, formerly No. 226 until its transfer from the mainland to the Isle of Wight.

No. W36, *Carisbrooke* (late No. 198), which, with No. W35 (late No. 181), was one of the last two transfers to the Isle of Wight, being sent over in 1949. They differ from the other Island engines in being motor fitted for pull-and-push working.

No. 30349 with original Adams' boiler.

No. 30160 as fitted with Drummond-type boiler.

No. 30397 as later fitted with Urie-type chimney and six wheeled tender.

No. 404 (30404) with original type of chimney and eight-wheeled tender, with which all the class were at one time fitted.

No. 30432, with original eight-wheeled tender and chimney.

No. 422 (allocated No. 30422 by British Railways but not renumbered), with Urie-type chimney, latterly fitted to most of the class. Ten of them also received six-wheeled tenders, as did this one.

No. 30464, with Urie chimney, as latterly fitted to most of the class. No. 30472, however, retained its Drummond chimney to the end, as in illustration of No. 30432 on the previous page.

A. F. Cook

No. 469 (30469), fitted with Maunsell boiler in 1925, the only one of the class so treated.

207

No. S316 (30316), as painted in first British Railways style.

No. 30334, Drummond 4–6–0, as rebuilt by Urie.

No. 30335, Drummond 4–6–0, as rebuilt by Urie.

No. 30489, Urie's first design of 4–6–0.

No. 30461, one of the only three of this class to receive its British Railways' number and livery.

No. 30452, *Sir Meliagrance*, one of Maunsell's first batch of 'King Arthurs'.

R. M. *Casserley*

No. 30458 'Ironside'.

No. 30475. The smoke deflectors were a later addition.

No. 30492 at Feltham. Originally stationed at Strawberry Hill, all the class were transferred to the new shed at Feltham in 1923, after the former shed was given over entirely to electric train storage.

No. 30497 at Woking. The class is occasionally used on express passenger work, particularly during the summer week-end traffic.

No. 30518. This class has occasionally been used for passenger duties on race days and other times of intensified working, but never with any regularity.

No. 30530 with wide chimney, with which the class was later fitted.

No. 30577 (late S.R. No. 3441) with Adams' tall dome.

No. 30571 (late S.R. No. 3397), with Adams' squat dome.

214

No. 30565 (late S.R. No. 3083), with S.E.C.R. class M3 boiler taken from a scrapped Kirtley 4–4–0 in 1929. Three or four of the class were so fitted about this period. This is one of the later engines with a longer front overhang.

No. 30570 (late S.R. No. 3167, the old number can be seen beneath the new), with Drummond-type boiler, as applied to one or two engines of the class.

R. M. Casserley

No. 30583 (late No. 3488), as fitted with Drummond boiler.

No. 30584 (late No. 3520), carrying Adams' boiler with squat dome. The boilers of these engines are sometimes interchanged, and a third variation is found in the form of an Adams' boiler with a tall dome (see comparative illustration on page 214).

No. 30585 (late S.R. 3314). This engine and No. 30587 have curved splashers.

No. 30586 (late No. 3329), with rectangular splashers.

217

No. 30588 (late No. 3741), originally built as a 2–2–0T.

No. 636, allocated No. 30636 but never carried. None of these engines acquired
their British Railways' number.

No. 756, *A. S. Harris*. This engine was allocated No. 30756 but never carried its new number.

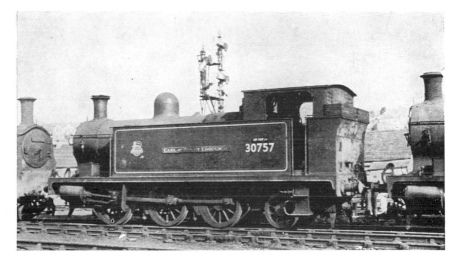

R. M. Casserley

No. 30757, *Earl of Mount Edgcumbe*.

No. 30753, *Melisande*, in first British Railways' style of painting.

No. 755 (30755), *The Red Knight*, with double blast pipe, as later fitted to engines 30736/7, 30741 and 30752/5.

No. 30789, *Sir Guy*, as first repainted in Southern Railway malachite green.

No. 30801, *Sir Meliot de Logres* with six-wheeled tender.

L. G. Marshall

No. 30840 with flat-sided eight-wheeled tender. Some of the class are now fitted with six-wheeled tenders and others with the earlier type of eight-wheeled tender as illustrated on page 212 by No. 30497.

No. 30863, *Lord Rodney.*

No. 30912, *Downside*, in original state with the exception of the later provision of smoke deflectors.

No. 30934, *St. Lawrence*, with multiple blast pipe and wide chimney later fitted to about half the class.

K. & E.S.R. No. 4. This previously independent line was acquired by British Railways in 1948. No. 4 was one of the two remaining engines; it was scrapped later in that year and was never allocated a British Railways' number.

30948

E.K.R.

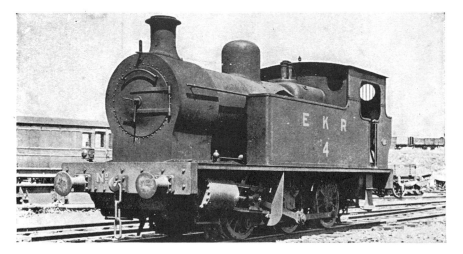

East Kent Railway No. 4. Allocated B.R. No. 30948, but scrapped in 1949 without being renumbered.

Southern Railway No. 949 Hecate, allocated No.30949 but scrapped in 1950 without being renumbered, shown here as first acquired by the S.R. in 1932. It afterwards received slight modifications including an enclosed safety valve.

No. 951 (30951). The unusual style of lettering was acquired whilst the engine was on loan to the War Department.

No. 31151, the only engine of this class to carry its British Railways' number.

No. 31446, the only engine of this class to carry its British Railways' number.

No. 31425, with leading sandboxes below the running plates, in common with the majority of the rebuilt engines.

East Kent Railway No. 6, allocated British Railways' No. 31372, but scrapped in 1949 without being renumbered. This engine was unique in retaining the original Stirling round cab. It also retained, as originally built, the smokebox wing plates allied to the front sandboxes above the running plates.

No. 1714 (later 31714), Wainwright 'Maid of All Work' class for the S.E.C.R. Except for the provision of shorter chimneys, the engines remained substantially as built.

No. 31555. These small engines had 3′9″ wheels and 12″ × 18″ cylinders.

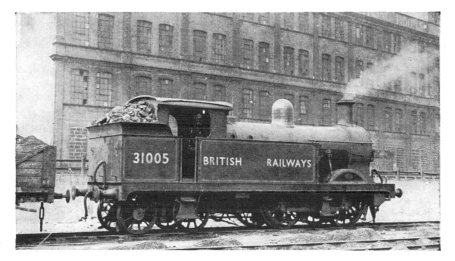

No. 31005. Wainwright standard passenger tank engine.

J. H. Aston

No. S1274 (31274), with flat-sided bunker, as found on a few of the class.

No. 31010, retaining the original round cab, and fitted with cut-down boiler mountings for working on the now defunct Canterbury & Whitstable line.

R. M. Casserley

No. 31069, another of the same class with original type of round cab, but with normal boiler mountings. Some of these engines had leading sandboxes below the running plates. Others (see lower illustration on p. 227) still retained the old position allied with smokebox wing plates.

No. 31047, with later type of cab. Most of these engines were employed working Boat Trains on the Folkestone Harbour Incline, sometimes with as many as three engines at the head of the train and a fourth banking. In 1959 they were replaced on these duties by G.W.R. 0–6–0PT's.

31302   S.E. & C.R. Crane engine

No. 1302, allocated No. 31302 but not carried. The crane jib was latterly out of use, and the engine finished its days shunting in the milk dock at Stewarts Lane.

R. M. Casserley

No. 31577, one of Wainwright's handsome early design of 1901. Apart from painting and the provision of shorter chimneys, the unrebuilt engines of this class remained substantially in their original condition until the end.

No. S1735 (31735), as completely rebuilt in 1921.

No. 31587, scrapped 1951. Nos. 31036 and 31275 were superheated, but remained unaltered in external appearances.

No. 31160 as rebuilt. The converted engines of classes D1 and E1 are largely identical, but it will be noted that class E1 has fluted side rods, whereas in class D1 (opposite) these are of plain section.

No. 31596. All five engines of this class were scrapped during 1950 and 1951.

No. 1602 (31602). Neither of the two engines in the capital stock received its British Railways' number. The service engine, No. 500S, was employed at Meldon Quarries.

No. 1661 (31661) in 1948, one of the last engines to retain the pre-war style of painting with large numerals.

No. 31703, fitted for pull-and-push working, to which most of the later survivors were adapted.

No. 31796, originally built as a 2–6–4T, *River Stour*.

No. S1631 (later 31631). The last ten of the class, Nos. 31630–9, had modified tenders with sloping tops.

No. 31890, formerly named *River Frome* before conversion to a tender engine.

No. 31894, 3-cylinder 2–6–0 express passenger engine.

No. 31869, one of the class built at Woolwich in 1921.

No. 1831 (31831), running in 1948 as an oil burner. This locomotive was subsequently reconverted to coal burning.

No. 1414 (31414), the last N class locomotive to be constructed.

No. 31879, Maunsell 3-cylinder 2–6–0.

No. 1685 (31685), originally built in 1900 as an 0–6–0 tender engine.

No. 31911, 3-cylinder 2–6–4T for freight work.

No. 31776, one of the German-built batch. Nos. 31772–31781 were built by Borsig of Berlin and delivered just prior to the outbreak of war in 1914.

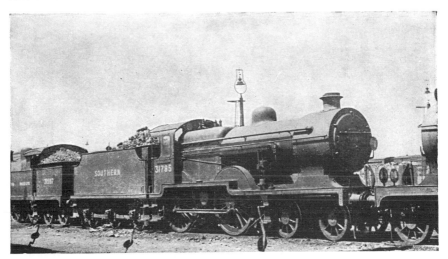

No. 31785, the last new design of inside cylinder 4–4–0 express engines in this country.

No. 32005, the only one of the class to acquire its British Railways' number.

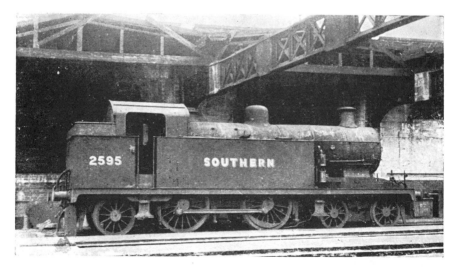

No. 2595, allocated No. 32595, but not carried. None of these engines were actually renumbered. They were similar to Nos. 32001–10, but with longer coupled wheelbase.

No. 2021 (32021), the original engine of the class with 6'9" driving wheels. The remainder have 6'7½" wheels. Illustrated with the flat-topped dome which was latterly fitted to most of the class.

No. 32086, with small dome and modified cab as fitted to the last engines of this class.

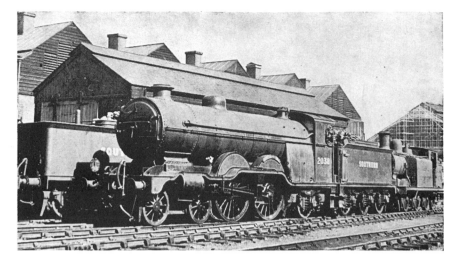

No. 2038, *Portland Bill*, scrapped in 1951 without being renumbered.

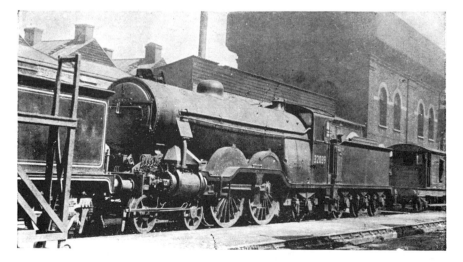

No. 32039, *Hartland Point*, which was used by Mr Bulleid for experimental purposes, shown as fitted with sleeve valves prior to the construction of his 'Leader' class, No. 36001. Never ran in ordinary traffic in its converted state, and scrapped in 1951.

R. M. *Casserley*

No. 32103, one of the original five engines, fitted with smaller side tanks.

No. 32105. This locomotive, together with Nos. 32106–9, was built with larger side tanks, in which the water capacity was increased from 1,090 to 1,256 gallons.

245

No. 2044 (32044) with flat-topped dome. None of the unrebuilt engines of this class acquired its British Railways' number.

No. 2068 (32068) with modified running plate. This engine is one of two which were lent to the L.N.E.R. during the war, and the shed code 'York', in that company's style, can still be seen on the buffer beam.

No. 32072, one of the few engines of this class which was repainted in fully lined-out B.R. livery.

Brighton 'Atlantic', No. 32421 *South Foreland.*

No. 2609 (32609), scrapped in 1948 with its old number and still carrying the original Stroudley boiler. The remainder all carried Marsh boilers, as in the illustration below.

No. W1, *Medina* (formerly No. 136), one of the four engines transferred to the Isle of Wight in 1932–3 and given names. They were fitted with L.S.W.R. Drummond-type chimneys.

No. 2160 (32160). None of these three engines was actually renumbered.

No. 32124, 0–6–2T rebuilt from Stroudley 0–6–0T class E1, illustrated opposite.

No. 2252 (32252), the last to remain in ordinary service. Motor fitted for pull-and-push working in common with most of the later survivors.

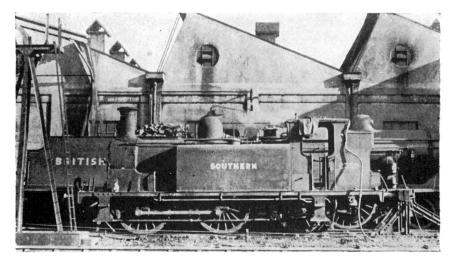

No. 2359 (32359) at Dover, in use as a stationary boiler in 1950. Withdrawn in 1951, this was the last of the class.

No. 2239 (32239), one of several which were fitted for fire fighting during the war. Scrapped in 1948 without being reconverted for ordinary service.

No. 2244, later renumbered 700S in the service list, one of two engines used for pumping oil fuel during 1946–8, when a number of locomotives were converted to oil burning. Scrapped in 1949.

No. 32303. Four of the class acquired their British Railways' numbers.

No. 2436 (32436). None of the engines of this class carried their new numbers.

No. 32546, rebuilt Vulcan 0–6–0.

No. 32440, one of the few engines of the class fitted with a second top-feed dome. The apparatus was latterly out of use, although the dome remained.

No. 2325 (32325), formerly named *Abergavenny*.

No. 32326, formerly named *Bessborough*.

No. 32333, *Remembrance*, the L.B.S.C.R. memorial engine of the First World War. The remainder of the class were named after famous locomotive engineers of the past.

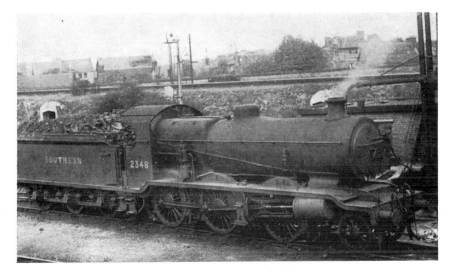

No. 2348 (later 32348). All of the class latterly carried the flat-topped dome.

No. 32384 with a pull-and-push train. Most of the later survivors were motor fitted.

No. 2397, scrapped in 1948 without receiving its new number.

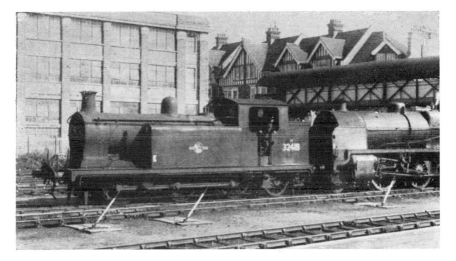

No. 32418, the last survivor, scrapped in 1963. These engines retained their original form to the end, even to the Billinton tapered chimney.

No. 32411 as rebuilt with larger boiler. See note on page 261 regarding engine No. 32407.

No. 2468 (32468), the last engine to retain the original short smokebox, it was rebuilt in 1949 in conformity with the rest of the class.

No. 32509 in the form in which most of the class later ran, although there were sundry variations in the boiler mountings.

No. 32480, with smaller dome and open Ramsbottom safety valves. Others of the class had enclosed Ramsbottom valves of the type illustrated opposite.

32466, 32477–8, 32489   L.B.S.C. Class E4X

No. 32466, as rebuilt with a larger boiler.

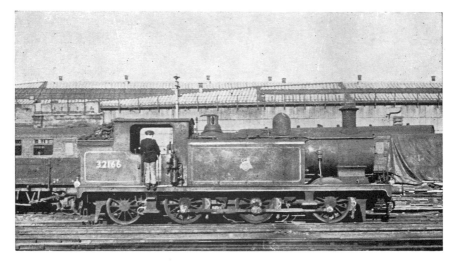

No. 32166. The boiler mountings of this class varied in the same way as in Class E4 (see previous page).

No. 32404, scrapped in 1951.

No. 32576, as rebuilt with large boiler.

No. 32401, carrying a boiler with a second dome formerly housing the top-feed apparatus. This boiler was formerly carried by No. 32407 of class E6X (see page 257).

No. 32670, one of the first two of the engines of this class. This engine, which still retains its Stroudley copper-capped chimney, and No. 32636 are the two oldest now in service on British Railways. Sold to Kent & East Sussex Railway in 1901 and returned to B.R. on Nationalisation as 32670 (having been originally L.B.S.C.R. No. 70).

No. 32644 in the form in which most of the survivors are now running. In contrast to No. 32670, which still retains the original sandboxes combined with splashers, it has the leading sandboxes below the running plate.

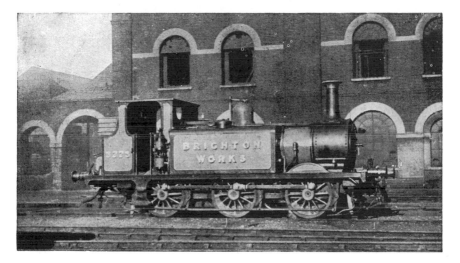

No. 377S, the Brighton Works' shunter. This locomotive was No. 2635 until 1946, when it was transferred to the service list and repainted in the original L.B.S.C.R. yellow livery, which it still retained in 1959. In that year it was re-transferred to the capital stock as No. 32635.

DS680   L.B.S.C. Class A1

The Lancing Carriage Works' shunter, which was sold to the S.E.C.R. in 1904 as No. 751, and became No. 680S in 1932.

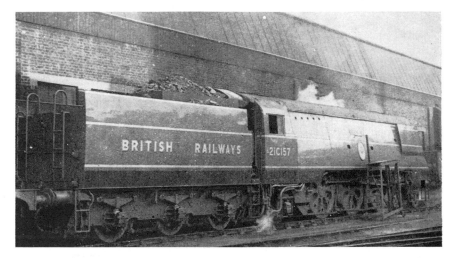

No. S21C157 (later 34057) *Biggin Hill* in original condition.

No. 34064, fitted with Giesl ejector and chimney, and with modified tender.

No. 34101 *Hartland*, as rebuilt in 1960.

No. 35026 *Lamport and Holt Line*, as rebuilt in 1957.

No. 35003, *Royal Mail*, in original condition.

No. 35021, *New Zealand Line*, one of the final ten with modified cab and tender, as first turned out in 1948.

266

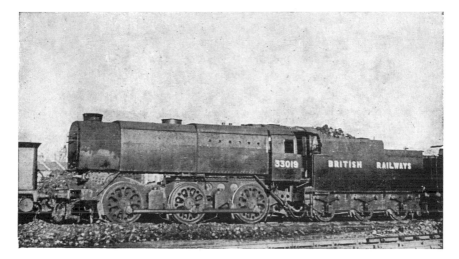

No. 33019, formerly No. C19. The class were turned out by the Southern Railway as Nos. C1-C40.

No. 36001, the only one of the class to run trials, but never placed in regular service.

THE LMS GROUP

No. 40001, with wide chimney and outside steam pipes, with which most of this class were later fitted.

No. 40010, fitted for pull-and-push working. As running with original arrangement of inside steam pipes and with earlier type of chimney.

271

No. 40 (40040), illustrating Nos. 40022–40040, stationed in the London area, and fitted with condensing apparatus for working through the Metropolitan line tunnels.

40071–40209　　　　　　　　　　　　　　　　　　Stanier 2–6–2T

No. M178 (40178), in first British Railways' style of numbering and painting.

J. R. Buckley

No. 40148 as rebuilt with larger boiler. The earlier engines of this class, Nos. 40071-40144, had domeless boilers.

40383, 40385, 40391   M. R. Johnson 4–4–0

No. 40383, the last surviving unsuperheated Midland 4–4–0, scrapped 1952.

273

Rebuilt Class 2 4-4-0 No. 40404, with original Johnson tender.

No. 40504, with Fowler tender as latterly fitted to the later survivors of this class. All formerly had the Johnson type, as in the illustration above.

No. M666 (40666), with original Fowler chimney. Most of the class later carried the Stanier type as illustrated below.

No. 633 (40633), fitted with 'dabeg' feed water heater. No. 40653 was similarly fitted.

No. 40743, Johnson class 3 4–4–0.

R. J. Buckley

No. 40726, showing the deeper framing found in some engines of this class.

No. 41009, in earlier standard British Railways' livery.

No. 1000 (withdrawn from ordinary service in 1951 as No. 41000), as restored in 1959 to full working order and in its former Midland Railway livery.

R. M. Casserley

No. 41167. This engine latterly ran with a taller chimney than the rest of the class. Most of them had the type carried by No. 41009, illustrated on the previous page, but some of those in Scotland still retained the Midland design shown on No. 936 below.

No. 936 (40936), as running with high-sided tender and original chimney. Only one of these tenders was fitted to any of these engines and for many years it was attached to No. 40936. It has recently, however, been transferred to engine 40933. No. 40934 retained the old L.M.S. red livery, as depicted in the above illustration, until March, 1949; it was probably the last engine to do so, none having been repainted in this colour after 1940.

278

No. 41229, with wide chimney and fitted for pull-and-push working.

No. 41312, non-motor fitted and with tall, narrow chimney.

No. 41516, one of the smaller series.

No. 41523, one of the last batch, of slightly larger dimensions and increased water capacity.

Nos. 1528 and 1529, with different arrangement of numbers and initials on the two engines. Now 41528 and 41529.

No. 41686, mainly in original condition, Johnson boiler with Salter safety valve and with half-section cab.

No. 41779, also retaining Johnson boiler, but rebuilt with all-over cab. This engine still carries the old Midland pattern chimney

R. M. Casserley

No. 41748, rebuilt with Belpaire boiler but retaining half-section cab. Others of the class have both Belpaire boilers and all-over cabs. This view shows the Dursley branch train at Coaley Junction.

No. 41909 at Watford on St. Albans motor train.

No. 41922, originally L.T. & S.R. 63, *Mansion House*, the last survivor of the 'Intermediate' 4–4–2T's.

No. 41950, originally L.T. & S.R. 44, *Prittlewell*.

R. M. Casserley

No. 41975, one of the later L.M.S.-built series of L.T. & S.R. Whitelegg design.

No. 1987 (41987), L.M.S. 2187 until 1947.

42050–42299, 42673–42699   Fairburn 2–6–4T

No. 2219, later 42219.

No. 42305, still with inside steam pipes. Most of the class later received outside steam pipes as in the illustration below. These engines were originally fitted with Midland chimneys of the type illustrated on engine M666 on page 275, but most or all have now been superseded by the later design illustrated.

No. 42424, rebuilt with outside steam pipes. The last thirty of the class, Nos. 42395–42424, have side window cabs as shown in this illustration.

No. 42590 as first renumbered. Early new smokebox door number plates were cast with figures in L.M.S. serif style, as in this illustration, but these have now been replaced by new ones with the later type of plain numbers.

No. 42509, 3-cylinder 2-6-4T specially designed for work on the Tilbury section.

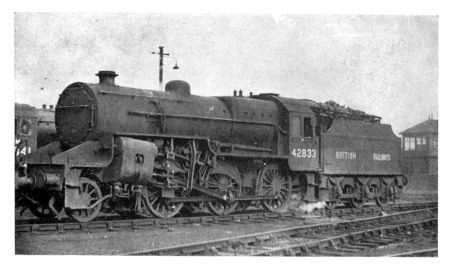

No. 42833, Horwich design of 2-6-0.

Five engines of this class, Nos. 42818, 42822, 42824, 42825, and 42829, were rebuilt in 1931 with Lenz poppet valves as here illustrated. They were again rebuilt in 1953 with Reidinger poppet valve gear.

No. 42956, as first repainted in early B.R. style.

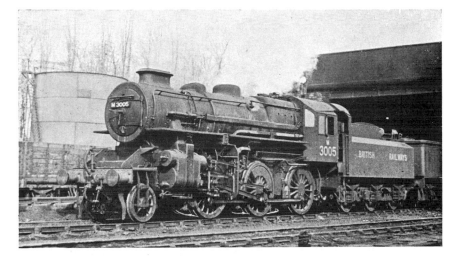

No. M3005 (43005), as originally built. The first fifty engines were constructed with double chimneys, but all were subsequently converted to single blast pipes and chimneys.

No. 43027, as experimentally fitted in 1953 with stove-pipe chimney.

No. 43152, illustrating Nos. 43050–43161, as built with single chimney, to which type the earlier engines were later altered.

No. M3186 (43186), rebuilt Johnson 4'11" 0-6-0.

Between 43191 and 43833

No. 43435, rebuilt Johnson 5'3" 0-6-0, with a unique type of tender. All other engines of the class carry the standard Johnson type, as in upper illustration.

No. 44000. Most of the Midland-built engines have the older type of tenders as shown above (many of these tenders being utilised from scrapped 2–4–0's and 4–2–2's). Some engines, however, have the later type shown below, and the tender cab appearing in the above illustration is to be found fitted to both varieties, although not a general feature.

44027–44606

No. 44497, with later standard Midland tender; but some of the L.M.S. built engines have the earlier design, and two or three of the last built are fitted with a high-sided type, as illustrated on page 298 with engine 45612.

No. 45156, *Ayrshire Yeomanry*, showing the class in its original form with domeless boiler. One of the only four of these engines to bear a name.

One of the later engines, M4763 (44763), as experimentally painted in L.N.E.R. green livery.

No. 44767, with Stephenson's outside valve gear, the only engine so fitted. It has a double chimney, which feature is also found on engines 44686/7, 44755–7 and 44765/6.

No. 44971, with self-weighing tender.

294

No. 44747, with Caprotti valve gear, low running plate and splashers, as fitted to engines 44738–44757.

W. H. Withworth

Nos. 44686 and 44687, the last two engines of the whole class to be constructed, were fitted with Caprotti valve gear and very high running plates, in accordance with modern B.R. practice.

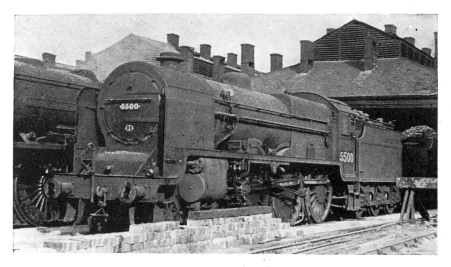

The first two engines, Nos. 45500/1, were nominally rebuilds of L.N.W.R. Claughton class engines, and actually retained the original wheels, distinguished by the large centre bosses as seen in the illustration.

No. 45520, *Llandudno*, illustrating the remainder of the class, which were entirely new engines, although up to 45541 were officially regarded as rebuilds.

No. 45545, as rebuilt with large taper boiler and double chimney and now classified 7P. Eighteen engines were thus dealt with and also Nos. 45735 and 45736 of the following class.

No. 5557 (45557), with M.R.-type Fowler tender, as carried by a few of the class. The majority have the standard Stanier type, as illustrated overleaf with No. 45742. Some carry domeless boilers similar to No. 45156 on page 293.

No. 45612, with an early type of flat-sided Stanier tender, as attached to a few of these engines.

No. 45742, fitted with a double chimney.

No. 6004, which nominally became 46004 in B.R. stock, but was scrapped without actually acquiring its new number.

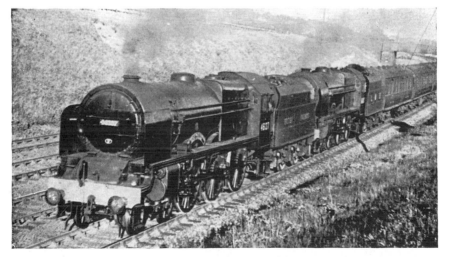

Nos. 46137 and 6110, both with original parallel boilers, near Berkhamsted. All of this class have now been rebuilt with taper boilers as in the illustrations of Nos. 46126 and 46170, No. 46137 being the last to be converted, in March, 1955.

No. 46126, as running with taper boiler. Rebuilding of these engines in this form commenced in 1943, at first without smoke deflecting plates, as in the illustration below (see also page 339). The deflectors were added from 1947.

46170

No. 46170, as rebuilt. It now carries smoke deflector plates and is practically identical with the rebuilt 'Royal Scot' class, as illustrated above.

No. 6211 (46211), *Queen Maud*, in immediate pre-Nationalisation style of painting as finally applied to L.M.S. express locomotives, and fitted with original type of domeless boiler. One or two of the class now carry domed boilers.

No. 46205, *Princess Victoria*, with modified valve gear.

No. 6202 (later 46202), turbine driven locomotive.

W. H. Whitworth

In 1952, No. 46202 was rebuilt as an ordinary 4-cylinder reciprocating locomotive and named *Princess Anne*. Its career in this condition was, however, destined to be very short, as it was involved in the disastrous Harrow accident on 8th October, 1952, and extensively damaged. It was never repaired and disappeared in Crewe works shortly afterwards, although not actually withdrawn from stock until May, 1954.

No. 46243, *City of Lancaster*, the last engine to retain the streamlining. No. 6226 was also in this condition at the beginning of 1948, but lost it during the year. No. 46243 was finally de-streamlined in June, 1949.

No. 6238 (46238), *City of Carlisle* as de-streamlined. The curved front to the smokebox was necessary to follow the contour of the streamlining, but these engines are now being fitted with straight-topped smokeboxes.

No. 46232, *Duchess of Montrose*, on Beattock bank.

No. 46257, *City of Salford*.

No. 46509, with wide chimney, repainted at Swindon in G.W.R. passenger green.

No. 46424, as experimentally fitted in 1951 with narrow stove-pipe chimney, and nicknamed 'the spout'.

No. 46474, with subsequent design of tall chimney. The last engines built of this class reverted to the former type of wide chimney shown on page 305.

No. 46666, one of the last survivors of a once numerous class, seen at Cheddington on the now defunct Aylesbury branch train.

No. 46762, L. & Y.R. type 2–4–2T, acquired from the Wirral Railway, built in 1890 and scrapped 1952.

Between **46876** and **46931**   L.N.W.R. 0–6–2T

No. 46900, the last survivor of the class, scrapped 1953.

R. M. Casserley

No. 47000 at work on the Cromford and High Peak Railway. The original
L.M.S. design of 1932.

47005–47009

R. M. Casserley

No. 47007, modified B.R. design, built 1953.

No. 47164, Fowler dock tank.

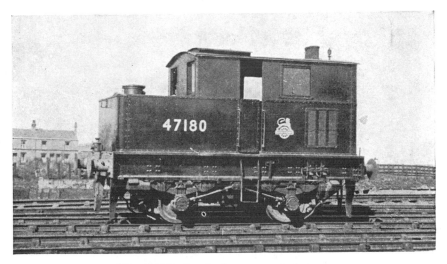

No. 47180, Sentinel two-speed shunter.

309

No. 47184, Sentinel single-speed shunter.

No. 7190 (47190), formerly S. & D.J.R. No. 101.

No. 47249, with condensing apparatus, with which the majority of the class were fitted for working in the London area through the Metropolitan line tunnels.

No. 47258, one of the engines built without condensing apparatus.

No. 47413, standard L.M.S. version of Johnson shunting tank engine.

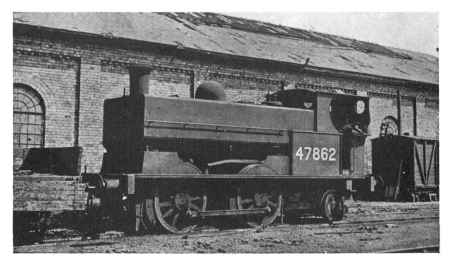

No. 47862, L.N.W.R. 'Box Tank'.

R. M. Casserley

No. 47877, the last survivor of the class, scrapped 1953.

R. M. Casserley

No. 47937, one of the last of the class to remain in traffic.

R. M. Casserley

No. 47994, with revolving bunker with which all but Nos. 47998–9 were subsequently fitted.

No. 4999 (later 7999 and finally 47999), with original bunker.

No. 48001, one of the original twelve engines with domeless boilers.

No. 8200 (48200), with domed boiler, as found on all but Nos. 48000–48011. Some of these engines later acquired Fowler tenders of the type illustrated on page 292 (lower), having exchanged them with engines of the 'Jubilee' class (pages 297-8).

No. M8602 (48602), as running for a short time during 1948 with a W.D.-type eight-wheeled tender. The change was in connection with the trials which took place during that year. S.R. engines were fitted with L.M.S. tenders for the trials over the northern lines, as their own had no water pick-up apparatus.

48801, 48824, 48834   L.N.W.R. 19″ goods

No. 8824 (48824). None of these engines was actually renumbered, all being scrapped as L.M.S. 8801, etc.

No. 48895, one of the earlier engines, originally a 2–8–0 compound. The whole class were practically identical with the one illustrated, although a few still retained L.N.W.R. chimneys as depicted in the lower illustration.

No. 9423 (49423), one of the final G2 class, Nos. 49395–49454, with round-topped firebox and L.N.W.R. chimney.

No. 49524, L.M.S. design of Fowler 0–8–0.

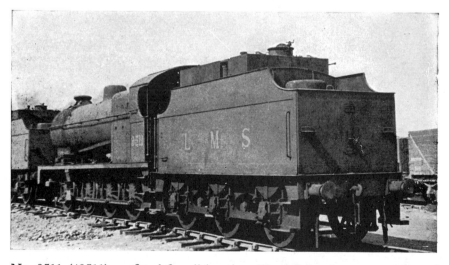

No. 9511 (49511), as fitted for oil burning. Five of the class were so treated in 1946–7, and four were broken up in 1949 without being reconverted. Only 49511 reverted to coal burning. Other classes, of which a few engines ran as oil burners during that period, were class 4 goods (43835), Class 5 4–6–0's (44658), and standard 2–8–0's (48000).

318

R. M. Casserley

No. 50455, the last survivor and the only one to receive its B.R. number.

50617   L. & Y.R. Rail Motor

R. M. Casserley

No. 10617 (50617), withdrawn in 1948 as L.M.S. 10617 without receiving its new number.

Nos. 50887 and 50731, both rebuilt with Belpaire fireboxes and extended smoke-boxes, showing varying sizes of bunker. Some of the class remained in their original form, as illustrated by No. 46762, page 307.

No. 50909, Hughes class 3 2-4-2T.

Nos. 11232 and 11231 (51232 and 51231). Engines of this class and the one shown on p. 322, stationed in Liverpool for working through the dock areas and streets, are fitted with spark-arresting device over the chimney, as illustrated.

No. 11394 (51394). Five of these engines were allocated to the Service Department for shunting in Horwich works, and all five retained their L.M.S. number.

No. 11535 (51535), fitted with spark arrester (see note on p. 321). The other three surviving engines of this class had ordinary spring buffers instead of the wooden ones as carried by this engine.

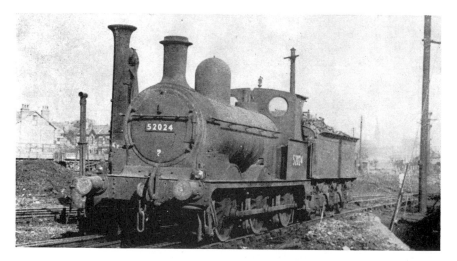

No. 52024, Barton Wright 0–6–0 of 1887.

R. M. Casserley

No. 52108, in practically original condition, as are the majority of the class.

No. 12104 (52104), rebuilt with Belpaire boiler and extended smokebox.

No. 52494, with original Furness type boiler.

No. 52501, rebuilt with L. & Y.R. boiler.

324

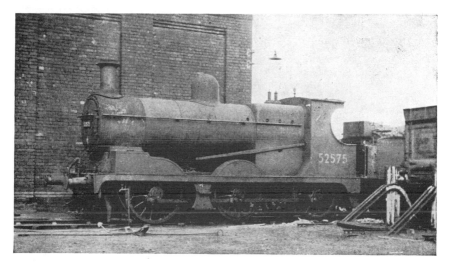

No. 52575, Aspinall 0–6–0 rebuilt by Hughes.

R. M. Casserley

No. 52727, the last surviving small-boilered 0–8–0, withdrawn 1950.

No. 52870, with earlier style cab.

No. 52857, with side window cab.

R. M. Casserley

No. 53800, the original smaller boiler version.

No. 53808, one of the later series with larger boilers. All have more recently carried the smaller boilers in conformity with the original 53800–53805 series.

No. 54450, in standard lined black livery.

54461–54508

No. 54481, the first of the class to be withdrawn.

R. M. Casserley

No. 14379 (54379), *Loch Insh.*

No. 54398, *Ben Alder*, the last of the class to remain in service.

No. 54399, *Ben Wyvis*, as fitted with stove-pipe chimney.

No. 54640, one of the L.M.S.-built series.

No. 54767, *Clan Mackinnon*, withdrawn January, 1950.

No. 55124, the last of the smaller C.R. McIntosh 0–4–4T's.

No. 55134, with the stove-pipe chimney, latterly carried by most of the class.

Between 55159 and 55240, and 55260 and 55269

No. 55260, one of the last ten, Nos. 55260-55269, which were put into service in 1925 after the grouping. It is illustrated here with the original Caledonian-type chimney.

No. 55051, one of the two H.R. tanks retained for working the Dornoch branch until replaced in 1957 by G.W.R. 0–6–0PT's.

No. M15352 (55352), as at first numbered in B.R. stock.

No. 56025, the C.R. 'Pug', the St. Rollox works shunter, painted in lined-out passenger livery.

No. 56020, as fitted with stove-pipe chimney.

No. 16153 (56153). Some of these engines now have stove-pipe chimneys similar to the other C.R. classes illustrated in these pages.

No. 56341, with original C.R.-type chimney.

No. 56254, with stove-pipe chimney, which many of these engines later acquired

The only class of engine of the former G. & S.W.R. to survive into B.R. days in 1948. No. 16905 was the last of the class and was scrapped in that year without being renumbered.

No. 57300, with original Caledonian-type chimney. This engine runs with
a tender from one of the McIntosh 4–6–0 Oban bogies, scrapped in the 1930's.
Most of the class have the standard type of tender shown in the lower illustration.

No. 57358, with stove-pipe chimney.

No. 57575, Caledonian McIntosh 0–6–0.

No. 57654, Caledonian Pickersgill 0–6–0.

No. 17693 (57693), Highland Railway 0–6–0 'Barney', together with rebuilt 'Royal Scot' No. 6103 (see page 300).

No. 17695 (57695), with original Drummond-type boiler, fitted with pop safety valves on dome.

A. G. Ellis

No. 57697, with C.R. boiler and stove-pipe chimney.

R. M. Casserley

No. 57955, seen here fitted with a snow-plough for winter working.

No. 25648, *Queen of the Belgians,* with round-topped boiler. This locomotive was allocated No. 58000, but the number was never carried.

No 25673, *Lusitania,* with Belpaire boiler (allocated 58001, but never carried).

341

No. 25297 (allocated 58010, but never carried), *Sirocco*, scrapped 1949.

R. M. Casserley

No. 25350, formerly named *India* (allocated No. 58011 but never carried).

No. 20155, allocated No. 58020, but never carried, shown here with older Midland-type chimney still to be found on some of the engines of the classes illustrated on these and the following pages.

No. 20185, allocated No. 58021, but never carried.

R. M. Casserley

No. 20216, allocated No. 58022, but never carried.

R. J. Buckley

No. 58092, late L.M.S. No. 26428.

L.M.S. No. 1252 (58035), with Johnson boiler, scrapped in 1950 without ever receiving its new number.

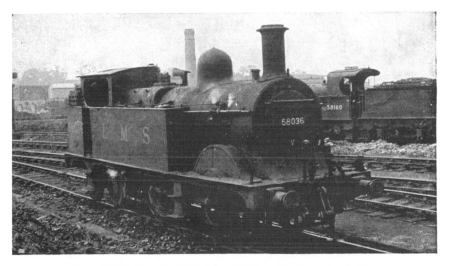

No. 58036 (late L.M.S. No. 1255), with Belpaire boiler.

No. 58051, with Johnson boiler.

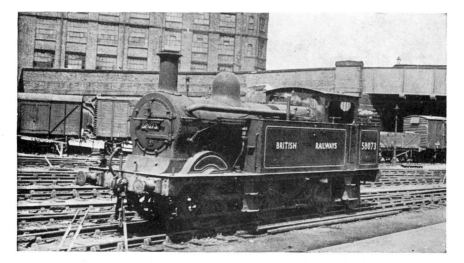

No. 58073, with Belpaire boiler. The illustration shows the condensing apparatus carried by some of the class, which formerly worked through the Metropolitan tunnels on the London suburban services.

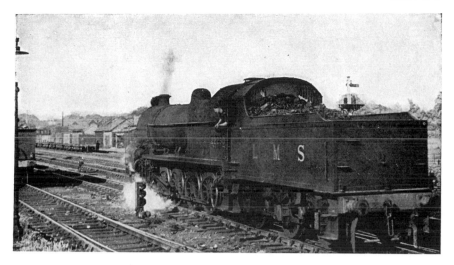

No. 22290 (58100), the Lickey Incline banker, nicknamed 'Big Bertha'.

No. 58110, late L.M.S. No. 22630, scrapped 1951.

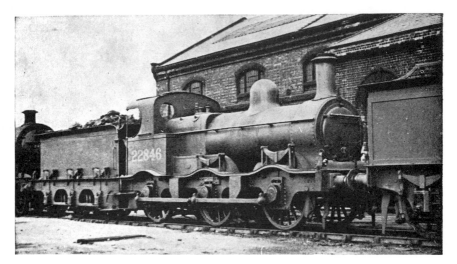

L.M.S. No. 22846 (allocated B.R. No. 58111).

No. 23011 (58183), with one of the 2,350 gallon tenders as carried until recent years by the earlier numbers of the class, later replaced by 2,750 gallon tenders, as shown in the succeeding illustrations.

No. 58302 (late L.M.S. No. 3691), with Belpaire boiler and Johnson cab.

No. 58213, with Belpaire boiler and Deeley cab. Also shown running with cab to tender, one of a very few engines so fitted.

R. M. Casserley

No. 58236 (late L.M.S. No. 3151) with Johnson boiler.

R. J. Buckley

No. 58238 (late L.M.S. No. 3156), with Belpaire boiler but retaining Johnson cab. Others of the class have Deeley cabs, as in the illustration of No. 58213.

350

R. M. Casserley

No. 58343 (late L.M.S. No. 28227), the last of a numerous and long-lived class. These engines were altered very little during the whole of their existence.

No. 58326 (late L.M.S. No. 28106), with unusual type of safety valve.

F. Jones

No. 58365 (late L.M.S. No. 28337), with original round-top boiler. Nearly all the later survivors, however, received Belpaire boilers as in the illustration below.

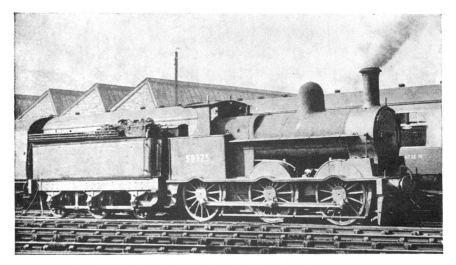

No. 58375 (late L.M.S. No. 28408), with Belpaire boiler.

R. J. Buckley

No. 58862 (late L.M.S. No. 27530), with original North London-type chimney.

No. 58853 (late L.M.S. No. 27512), with L.N.W.R. chimney.

353

R. M. Casserley

No. 58865 (late L.M.S. No. 27217), N.L.R. crane tank.

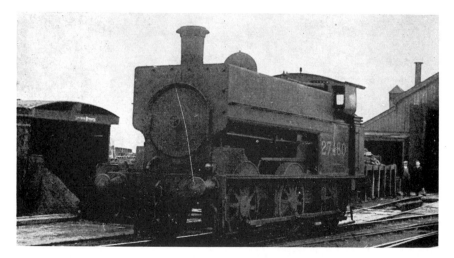

No. 27480 (allocated B.R. No. 58870, but never carried). Scrapped in 1948.

No. 58903 (late L.M.S. No. 7711). Almost the whole of this class remained practically unaltered throughout their existence.

No. 58916 (late L.M.S. No. 7759), one of the few exceptions, which received widened side tanks.

No. 3323, shunter at Crewe works. The number carried is the former L.N.W.R. one; it was never renumbered either by the L.M.S. or B.R., but the latter numbered it 43323 in error for a short time in 1949. Built 1878; scrapped 1954.

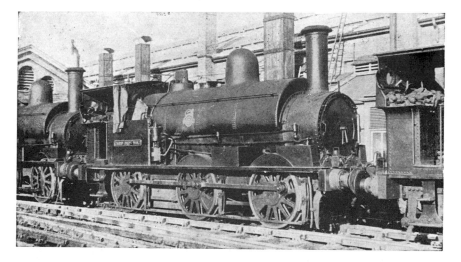

R. M. Casserley

Four similar engines were employed at Wolverton carriage works, C.D. Nos. 3, 6, 7, and 8, built 1875–9. Shown here is No. 6, with Westinghouse brake.

R. M. Casserley

Wren, the Horwich narrow gauge works engine.

L.N.W.R. rail motor No. 29988 (coaching stock number; these were never numbered in the locomotive series).

The first 4–6–0 in Great Britain, as running in 1959 after restoration.

The Caledonian Railway single, now restored to its original condition.

THE L.N.E.R. GROUP

No. 60034, *Lord Faringdon* with Kylchap blast pipe double chimney. The
majority of the class had single chimneys, as in the illustration below.

No. 13 (60013), *Dominion of New Zealand*, showing the corridor tender with
which most of the class were fitted. They were introduced by Sir Nigel Gresley
to provide communication with the train, making a change of crew possible
on long non-stop runs.

No. 60037, *Hyperion*. Some of these locomotives had a G.N.R.-type tender with coal rails, while others had the later L.N.E.R. design as in the illustration opposite. The majority of the class were latterly fitted with double chimneys.

No. E103 (60103), *Flying Scotsman*, showing the banjo-shaped dome which many of the class carried.

362

No. 60097, *Humorist*, with Kylchap blast-pipe and smoke deflectors. The only engine of the class so fitted.

No. 68 (60068), *Sir Visto*, the only Gresley 'Pacific' still running in 1948 in unrebuilt form as class A10 (formerly known as class A1), with 180 lbs. boiler pressure. It was later rebuilt to class A3 with standard 220 lbs. pressure.

J. O. Templeton

No. 60046 Diamond Jubilee, showing the small smoke deflectors with which these engines were later fitted. In common with many others of the class it also has a double chimney.

No. 60113, *Great Northern*, the original Gresley 'Pacific' of 1922, as rebuilt in 1945 to class A1/1 and forming the prototype to class A1 (opposite).

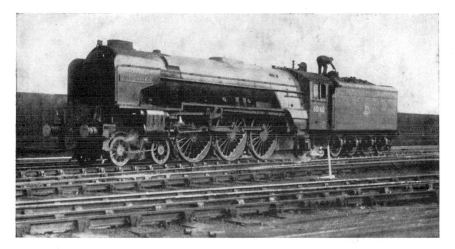

No. 60160. *Auld Reekie*, with original chimney. These locomotives at first ran without names.

No. 60158, later named *Aberdonian*, with the later type of lipped chimney.

Jayne Templeton

No. 60518 *Tehran,* as later running with lipped chimney. These engines originally had plain chimneys as in the illustration of No. 60160 (page 365).

No. 60503, *Lord President.* These were originally constructed as 2-8-2 engines.

F. M. Gates

No. 60508, *Duke of Rothesay.*

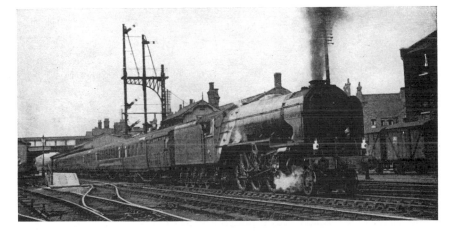

No. 525 (60525), *A. H. Peppercorn.* Some of the engines of this class have double blast pipes and chimneys.

No. 60700, formerly No. 10000, Britain's only 4–6–4 tender locomotive and in its day the most powerful passenger engine.

No. 60827, Gresley 'Green Arrow' mixed traffic class. Some of these engines have double blast pipes and chimneys.

No. 61037, *Jairou*. One of the original forty of the class named after South African antelopes.

No. 1355 (allocated British Railways No. 61355 but never carried). None of these engines survived to be renumbered.

No. 1362 (allocated No. 61362 but not carried), one of the earlier 1921–2 series of this class.

No. 1393 (allocated No. 61393 but not carried), one of the later post-grouping engines built in 1923–4.

No. 61477, Raven 4-6-0 in original condition.

No. 61464, one of the rebuilt engines.

No. 1475 (61475). This locomotive together with No. 61469 were the only two of the class to receive new numbers.

No. 1482, *Immingham*, which was allocated No. 61482, although none of the class actually carried their new numbers.

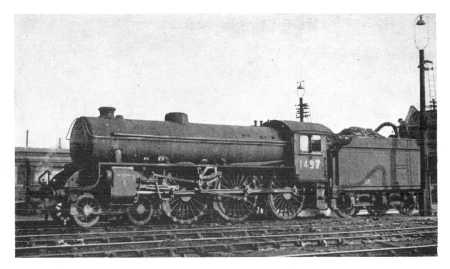

No. 1497, scrapped in 1949 as No. 61497.

No. 1680 (allocated No. 61680). None of these engines actually carried their
new numbers.

No. 61560, with original Great Eastern type of Belpaire boiler.

No. 61508, with round-topped boiler fitted to some engines from 1943 onwards.

No. E1555 (No. 61555), as rebuilt by Gresley to class B12/3.

British Railways

No. 1699, used from 1934 to 1951 as a counter pressure engine for testing purposes at Darlington works and later at Rugby.

No. 61600 *Sandringham*, the original 3-cylinder design.

No. 61644, *Earlham Hall*, as rebuilt with two cylinders.

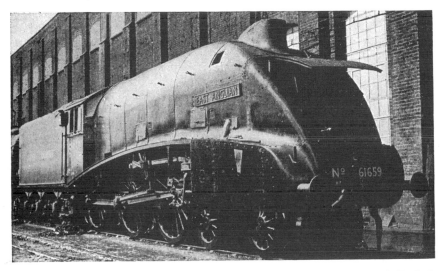

A. F. Cook

No. 61659, *East Anglian*, with streamlined casing. No. 61670 was similarly fitted, but the streamlining was later removed from both locomotives.

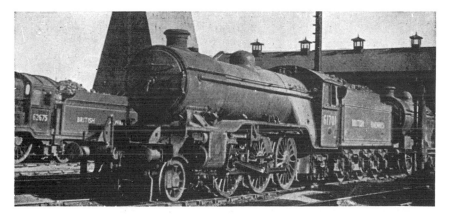

No. 61701, unofficially known as 'Bantam Hen'. No. 61700 bore the nameplate *Bantam Cock*.

No. 61721, Gresley 2-cylinder 2–6–0.

No. 61791. *Loch Laggan*, one of several of the class transferred to Scotland shortly after grouping for working on the West Highland line. These locomotives were fitted with side window cabs and named after Scottish lochs.

No. 1935 (No. 61935), Gresley large-boilered 3-cylinder 2–6–0, repainted in L.N.E.R. green.

E. R. Wethersett

No. 1863 (No. 61863), rebuilt with two cylinders.

No. 61995, *Cameron of Lochiel*, Gresley's 3-cylinder 2–6–0 for the West Highland line.

No. 61997, *MacCailin Mor*, rebuilt with two cylinders.

No. 62027, one of the new K1 locomotives built in 1949 on the lines of the rebuilt No. 61997 (see lower illustration on opposite page).

Between **62059** and **62072** (survivors renumbered   Class D31
62281–3 on construction of class K1 above)

R. M. Casserley

No. 62060, later No. 62282, Holmes 4–4–0.

No. 2112. Neither of these locomotives bore their British Railways' number, both being scrapped in 1948. No. 2111 carried the old North Eastern type brass column safety valve.

No. 62000, Great Northern 4–4–0 rebuilt with side window cab and employed principally for hauling officers' saloons.

No. 2140, allocated No. 62140 but withdrawn as British Railways' No. E2140.

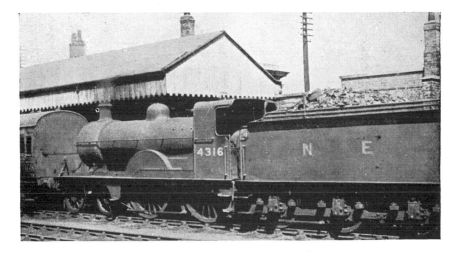

No. 62131, formerly L.N.E.R. No. 4316, which differed from all other locomotives of this class in having two separate splashers.

No. 62172, scrapped in 1951, was the last G.N.R. 4–4–0 locomotive to remain in service.

No. 2199, allocated 62199 but not renumbered, with superheater and extended smokebox.

No. 62228, Great North of Scotland 4–4–0 design by James Johnson.

No. 62270, one of the earlier unsuperheated series.

No. 2276 (No. 62276), *Andrew Bain*, fitted with superheater, as were all the later engines of this series.

49

No 49, *Gordon Highlander* (late 62277), as restored in 1959 to its former G.N.S.R. livery and now in working order.

No. 62307, *Queen Mary*, one of the four engines of the class which were originally given names.

No. 2384 (No. 62384), with original North Eastern type of smokebox. Some
of the locomotives of this class ran with L.N.E.R. flat-sided tenders.

R. M. Casserley

No. 62360, with later type of smokebox. This locomotive, together with Nos. 62349, 62371 and 62375, have also been rebuilt with long travel piston valves and reclassified D20/2, but only No. 62349 (see below) was radically different in appearance from the rest of the class.

62349

Class D20/2

No. 62349, rebuilt with piston valves and raised framing, the only locomotive so treated.

No. 62411, *Lady of Avenel*, repainted in L.N.E.R. green.

No. 62437, *Adam Woodcock*, one of the later 'Scott' series.

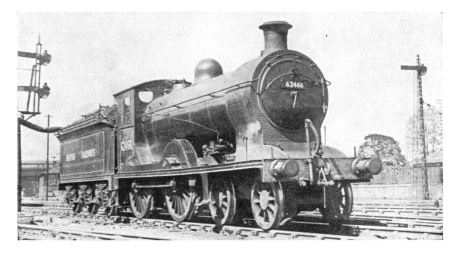

No. 62466, class D33. Class D32 was almost identical in appearance.

No. 62478 *Glen Quoich.*

No. 256, *Glen Douglas* (late 62469), in full working order and restored to its former N.B.R. condition.

R. M. Casserley

No. 62508, one of the last remaining unconverted 'Claud Hamiltons'. The G.N.R. pattern chimney was fitted in the 1930's.

H. D. Hewitt

No. 62507 (formerly L.N.E.R. No. 8896), which differed from the others of this class in having had the decorative framing over the coupling rods removed. This locomotive also has one of the Holden tenders originally constructed for oil burning engines.

No. 62547, rebuilt 'Super Claud' with larger boiler.

No. 62605, rebuilt with Gresley round-topped boiler, but retaining the old decorative framing.

No. 62614 with Gresley round-topped boiler and cut-away splashers. Painted in L.N.E.R. green, this locomotive, together with No. 62618, was for many years used for hauling Royal trains.

No. 62659, *Worsley Taylor*, one of the original Great Central 'Directors'.

No. 2664 (No. 62664), *Princess Mary,* one of the second batch of 'Directors' with side window cabs and other modifications.

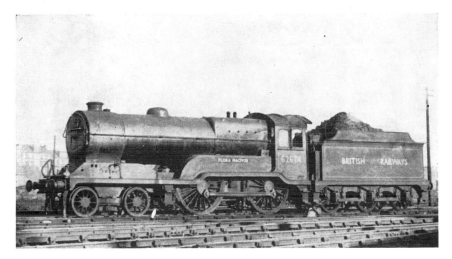

No. 62674, *Flora MacIvor*, one of the 1924 series of 'Directors' with cut-down boiler mountings for service in Scotland.

No. 62714, *Perthshire*, Gresley 2-cylinder 'Shire' class with Walschaert's valve gear, fitted with a tender from a former North Eastern engine. Some of the locomotives of this class had Great Central tenders.

No. 62739, *The Badsworth*, Gresley 3-cylinder 'Hunt' class with Caprotti valve gear. A variety of tenders were fitted both to these locomotives and those of the 'Shire' class.

No. 62768, *The Morpeth*, 'Hunt' class rebuilt with two inside cylinders, the only one of the series so treated.

No. 62780, retaining earlier G.E.R. pattern of stovepipe chimney.

No. 62790, in the form in which most of the latter-day survivors ran. This locomotive also acquired the lined-out passenger livery.

No. 62784, one of six engines which worked on the N.E.R. between Darlington and Penrith for a time during the 1930's and were fitted with side window cabs to make them more suitable for this exposed line. This locomotive is also seen with a somewhat shorter chimney and is here running with one of Holden's round-topped tenders designed for oil burning.

No. 62822, Ivatt 'Atlantic', the last of the class in ordinary service and one of the only two to receive its British Railways' number.

No. 2808 (No. 62808), rebuilt in 1917 as a 4-cylinder locomotive, but reconverted to a 2-cylinder engine in 1938. It retained the higher running plate it acquired at its first rebuilding. Scrapped in 1948.

No. 62849 (shown here with its former number 4419), rebuilt in 1923 with booster to the trailing wheels, later removed. It received its side window cab at the same time. Scrapped in 1948 as No. 2849.

No. 2908 (No. 62908). None of this class carried its allocated British Railways' number.

R. J. Buckley

No. 62937, shown here with its former number 1792. Withdrawn in 1948 as No. 2937, neither survivor receiving its British Railways' number.

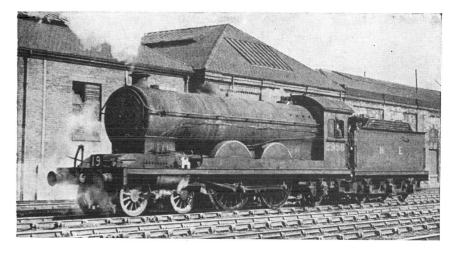

No. 2958, taken out of service in 1947. British Railways' numbers were never carried by any engines of this class.

No. 63188, as it ran for a short time, later renumbered 90509.

No. 3219 (No. 63219). A few locomotives of this class received their British Railways' number.

No. 3240 (No. 63240), one of the later engines of the class with continuous rear splasher.

A. F. Cook

No. 63333, one of the few engines of this class to acquire its British Railways'
number.

No 3325, rebuilt with boiler from Hull and Barnsley 0–8–0 and illustrated
with its former number 661. This engine was scrapped in 1947.

No. 63346, the middle variation of North Eastern 0–8–0's.

No. 63460, the largest class of North Eastern 0-8-0 engines with 3-cylinders.

No. 63489, illustrated with its former L.N.E.R. number 3471. It was withdrawn in 1948 as No. 3489. Most of this class, however, received their British Railways' number.

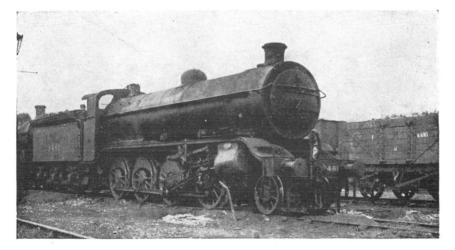

W. H. Whitworth

No. 63921, shown here with its former L.N.E.R. number 3461, and in the earlier style of painting. Scrapped in 1948 as No. 3921.

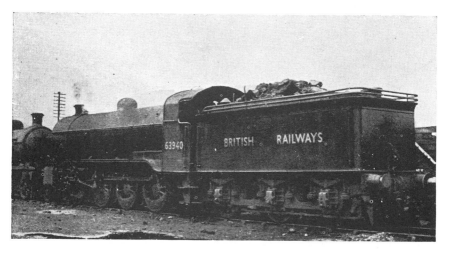

No. 63940, with G.N.R. pattern of cab and tender.

No. 63983, one of the later locomotives with side-window cab and L.N.E.R. design of tender. Some of the original Great Northern series also had side-window cabs, while others received B1-type boilers.

No. 63666, the original design of Robinson 2–8–0, now sub-classified O4/1.

No. 63920, one of the final series with side-window cab, sub-classified O4/6.

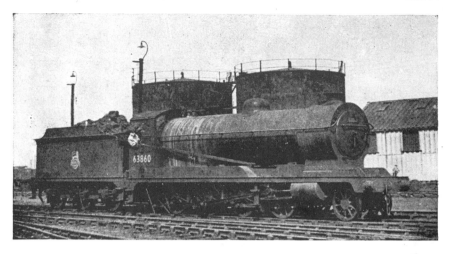

No. 63860, rebuilt with round-topped boiler and reclassified O4/7.

No. 63893, rebuilt with B1-type boiler and side-window cab, but retaining the original cylinders, framing and splashers (Class O4/8). Another variation, class O4/5, was very similar in appearance but did not carry the side-window cab.

No. 63777, Thompson rebuild of Robinson 2–8–0.

R. J. Buckley

No. 64141, rebuilt Ivatt 0–6–0.

409

No. 64109, seen here with its former L.N.E.R. number 4040, was scrapped in 1949 as No. 4109. This is one of the older Stirling-built engines, distinguishable from the later Ivatt ones in the different arrangement of sandboxes on the splashers. This locomotive also carries the original Stirling round cab, modified with a top extension to the rear. Most of the Stirling engines received the flatter Ivatt pattern of cab.

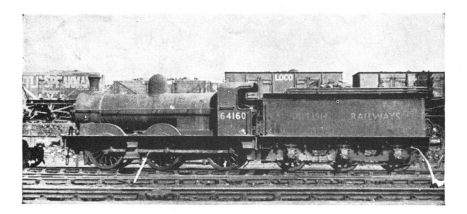

No. 64160, with shorter chimney and extended smokebox. This locomotive was formerly M. & G.N.J.R. No. 85 and was the only engine from that railway to be repainted 'British Railways' and to carry its new number.

410

R. M. *Casserley*

No. 64260. The earlier engines of this class did not have the leading sandboxes combined with the front splashers.

R. M. *Casserley*

No. 64413, unrebuilt class J11 G.C.R. 0–6–0.

411

No. E4379 (No. 64379), rebuilt with piston valves and higher-pitched boiler.

No. 64499, North British 'Intermediate' 0–6–0.

No. 64536, North British large 0–6–0.

No. 64646, Great Eastern Hill 0–6–0 rebuilt with Gresley boiler.

No. 4689 (No. 64689), Hill's largest design of 0–6–0 as built with Belpaire firebox. All have now been converted to class J20/1.

No. 64687, as rebuilt with round-topped boiler.

No. 64845, Gresley's standard mixed traffic 0–6–0, was fitted with a tender from a former North Eastern engine, but most of the class had standard L.N.E.R. flat-side tenders, as is the case with the second engine of the class seen in the background. Some were fitted with Westinghouse brakes.

Between **65002** and **65014**   Class J1

No. 5005 (No. 65005), Ivatt 5'8" mixed traffic 0–6–0. The domes and chimneys of these engines latterly varied a good deal: some had shorter chimneys and smaller domes, strongly resembling No. 65016 (following page), whilst No. 65009 had a long chimney but very squat dome and was similar in appearance to No. 65497 (see page 420).

R. M. Casserley

No. 65016, larger Gresley superheated version of class J1.

No. 65199, Parker design of M.S. & L.R. 0–6–0. This engine has Ross pop safety valves, but some of the class still retained the old Ramsbottom type. The tenders fitted to this class varied in size.

No. 5118 (No. 65118), unsuperheated Worsdell 5′1″ 0–6–0.

No. 65098, with superheater and extended smokebox.

417

No. 65217, *French*, one of the engines which served in France during the First World War.

No. 65287, which, together with No. 65285 (seen in background), had a cut-down chimney and boiler mountings for working on the Glenbeigh branch.

No. 65447, typical of most of the later survivors. A few still carried the old stovepipe chimney (see illustration of 2–4–0, No. 62780, on page 397).

No. 65424, with side-window cab for working on the Colne Valley line. Nos. 65391, 65405, 65432 and 65438 were similarly fitted.

No. 65497, in the form in which most of the class ran in their later days, although the chimneys and domes varied amongst different engines. Nos. 65480 and 65489 were superheated.

No. 5494 (No. 65495), with very squat dome. No. 65490, on the other hand, had a standard-size dome and shorter chimney, similar in appearance to No. 65016 (page 416).

No. 5644 (allocated No. 65644 but not carried), with extended smokebox. This engine retained the old North Eastern type of safety-valve column, although most of them had acquired pop safety valves. A number of the class had been fitted with piston valves and some of them were also superheated.

R. M. Casserley

No. 65655, unsuperheated and with slide valves. The same variations in this class apply as to class J24 (above). This locomotive is seen fitted with a snow-plough for working on the Darlington-Kirkby Stephen line.

Nos. 65746 and 65745, showing two of the varying styles of chimneys and domes found on this class.

No. 65869, fitted with superheater and extended smokebox. The majority of the class were unsuperheated and had short smokeboxes as in class J26 (above).

No. 65506, with small tender. Most of this class were fitted with the larger tender as found on the 'Claud Hamilton' 4–4–0's (see page 391).

No. 65905, rebuilt with boiler standard to class J39. Class J38 engines were built with 6″ longer boilers and correspondingly shorter smokeboxes, many remaining in this condition.

No. 7094 (allocated No. 67094 but not carried), awaiting cutting up. Neither
locomotive of this class acquired its British Railways' number.

No. 7111 (No. 67111), fitted for pull-and-push working, in common with others
of these classes. Classes F1 and F2 were similar in appearance.

No. 7137 (67137) with stovepipe chimney and Ramsbottom safety valves. The boiler mountings in this class, also F4, F5 and F6, vary considerably.

No. 7164 (No. 67164), with new number plate on smokebox but not yet re-numbered on tank sides. This was one of two locomotives fitted with a cow-catcher for working the St. Combs branch in Scotland. See note under class F3 regarding variations in boiler mountings.

No. 67193, repainted in lined-out livery. Some of this class were fitted for pull-and-push working. See note under class F3 regarding variations in boiler mountings. This engine has Pop safety valves.

No. 67203, fitted with condensing apparatus, as applied to a number of this class.

No. 67227. Two of this class, Nos. 67218 and 67219, were rebuilds from class F4 and retained the smaller-sized tanks of that class, although acquiring side-window cabs as found on class F6. See note under class F3 regarding variations in boiler mountings.

No. 7279 (No. 67279), with bunker as originally constructed. Many of the class were fitted for pull-and-push working.

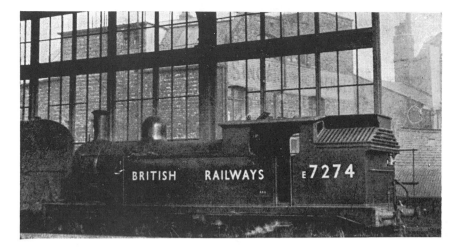

No. E7274 (No. 67274), with increased coal capacity as later fitted to most of the class, some with additional hopper-type extension as shown on this locomotive, and some without as in the lower illustration.

No. 67340, as running with its former L.N.E.R. number 387, and with extended side tanks, the only one of the class so modified.

No. 7353 (No. 67353), one of the original ten of the series, not fitted with condensing apparatus, as were subsequent engines of the class. Note the unusual
design of chimney. Most of the class have a Great Northern built-up type
carried by many of the later engines. Several were fitted for pull-and-push
working.

No. 67375, retaining short chimney, but condensing apparatus removed. The
later 50 engines differed from the first ten in having flared-out bunkers, as can
be seen in comparative illustrations.

No. E7422 (No. 67422), one of the Robinson earlier 4–4–2T's, some of which were fitted for pull-and-push working.

No. 67451, with large lettering on side tanks, a style at first adopted by Gorton under the British Railways' regime.

No. 67455, as first renumbered with L.N.E.R.-style numerals. Nos. 67460 and 67474 were adapted for pull-and-push working.

No. 67499, larger superheated version of class C15.

Jayne Templeton

No. 67610, one of the original V1 class engines.

No. 67672, rebuilt as class V3. This engine had a modified bunker, and at the time the photograph was taken was fitted with Westinghouse brake for working on the Great Eastern section.

No. E9011, as first numbered when built, later becoming No. 67712. From No. 67730 onwards the engines had the running plate cut away in front of the piston valves.

No. 68035, wartime austerity-type 0–6–0ST, built for the War Department. Many of the class later acquired the hopper-type bunker.

No. 68081 seen here with its former L.N.E.R. number 7230. Withdrawn in 1948 as No. 8081.

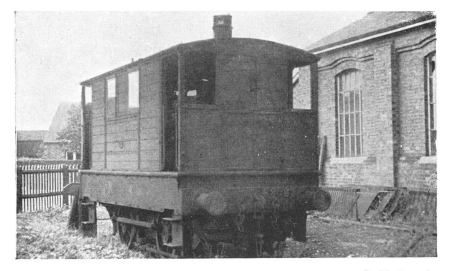

R. M. Casserley

No. 68082. Great Eastern 4-wheeled tram engines.

A. F. Cook

No. 68088 as Stratford works shunter.

No. 8091, later renumbered 55 in the Departmental stock.

No. 68100, seen here with auxiliary 4-wheeled tender; these were frequently attached to Class Y9 locomotives. This one spark had a arrester to the chimney.

No. 8123 (No. 68123), not fitted with the tall safety-valve column normally found on this class.

No. 68126, Hill G.E.R. 0–4–0T. The coal rails in front of the cab are a fairly recent addition. No. 68129, which was renumbered 33 in the Departmental list in 1953, latterly acquired a G.N.R.-type chimney.

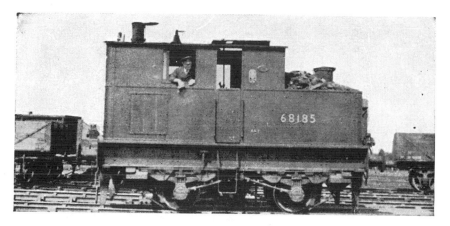

R. M. Casserley

No. 68185, class Y3 Sentinel shunting locomotive with 2-speed gear. Class Y1 had only a single speed, but the two classes are identical in appearance.

437

No. 68186, double-ended super-Sentinel locomotive.

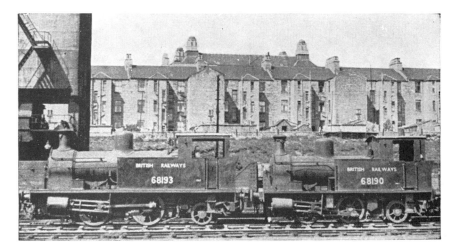

Nos. 68193 (class Z5) and 68190 (class Z4).

No. E8200 (No. 68200), Pollitt 0–6–0ST.

No. 68207, Robinson side-tank version of class J62.

No. 8215, which was allocated No. 68215 but scrapped in 1949 without being renumbered.

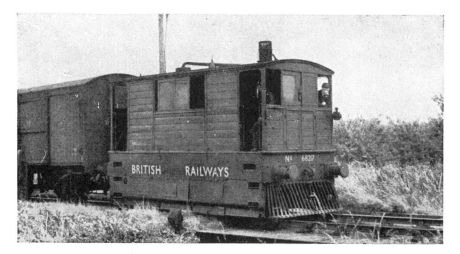

No. 68217, Great Eastern 6-wheeled tram engine.

No. 68286, painted in L.N.E.R. green for station-pilot duties at York.

No. 68317, illustrated here with its former L.N.E.R. number 3859. Taken out of service in 1948 as No. 8317.

No. 68339, still carrying the original-type boiler with pop safety valves on dome.

No. 68330, with the type of boiler which the majority of these locomotives afterwards carried.

No. 68345, as afterwards fitted with stove-pipe chimney.

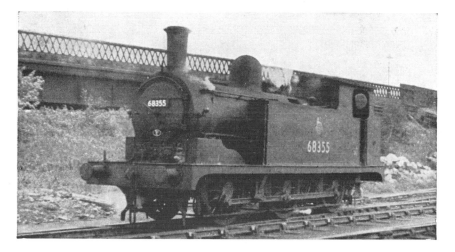

No. 68355, the larger class of North Eastern 0–6–0T.

C. Smith

The last surviving Hull & Barnsley 0–6–0T, seen here with its former L.N.E.R. number 2532. Scrapped in 1949 as No. 8365.

No. 8366, allocated No. 68366, but withdrawn during 1948 without ever being renumbered.

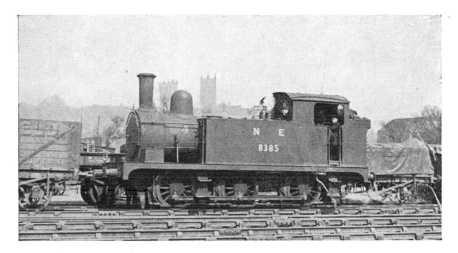

No. 8385 (No. 68385). Some of these locomotives carried the old type of stove-pipe chimney, as illustrated by No. 68577 (see page 448).

No. 68429, one of the York rebuilds, all of which retained the original round cab.

No. 8404 (No. 68404), one of the class rebuilt at Darlington, which were given Worsdell cabs.

No. 8477 (No. 68477), which, with two or three others, was painted light green by the L.N.E.R., in that Company's last year, for station-pilot work at Edinburgh Waverley.

No. 8488, allocated No. 68488, but scrapped in 1948 without receiving its new number. None of the class survived to be renumbered. No. 8484 had a stove-pipe chimney.

No. 68520, class J67/1, as first renumbered with L.N.E.R. style of numerals.

447

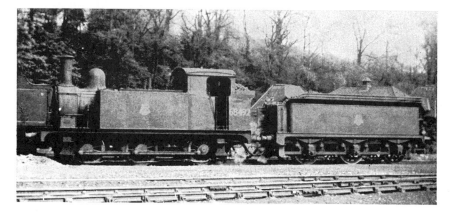

R. M. Casserley

No. 68492, class J67/2, fitted with auxiliary tender for working the Lauder branch from Galashiels. To reduce the axle load the side tanks were left empty. No. 68511 was similarly fitted.

No. 68577, class J69, still carrying the stove-pipe chimney as originally fitted to these engines. Most of the class later carried the lipped chimney. In 1959 No. 68619, used on station pilot duties at Liverpool Street, was repainted in the G.E.R. dark blue livery.

No. 68666, the final class of Great Eastern 0–6–0T, with side-window cab.

No. 8667 (No. 68667), 0–6–0T crane engine.

No. 68736, which together with No. 68723 was latterly painted in the old
N.E.R. light green for station pilot work at Newcastle. They carry the N.E.R.
crest and the new British Railways emblem.

No. 68709, a class J72 locomotive which worked in Scotland for some years and
acquired a stove-pipe chimney at Cowlairs.

450

No. 68795, a Stirling engine which acquired a stove-pipe chimney. Most of the class had the normal pattern as illustrated below. The small casing between the dome and the chimney is part of the condensing apparatus.

No. 68888, Ivatt development of the Stirling 0–6–0ST's. Small differences, such as the flared top to the bunker, will be noted in comparison with the Stirling locomotive illustrated above.

451

No. 68955, representing the appearance of the majority of the class. The earlier
G.N.R.-built engines had slightly more rounded cabs and otherwise differ
slightly in minor details.

No. 8981 (No. 68981), illustrating Nos. 68978–68991, fitted with larger bunkers.

No. 9053 (allocated No. 69053 but scrapped in 1950 without being renumbered), with earlier flower-pot chimney. Several of this class survived to receive their British Railways' numbers.

No. 9059 (allocated No. 69059 but withdrawn in 1949 without receiving its British Railways' number), with altered bunker and later type of chimney with which most of the class were finally fitted.

No. 9071, allocated No. 69071 but not carried. Both locomotives were taken out of service in 1948 without receiving their new numbers.

No. 9076, *Robert H. Selbie*, allocated No. 69076 but not carried. The other locomotive, No. 9077, *Charles Jones*, was also scrapped without being renumbered, both engines being withdrawn in 1948.

No. 9089, allocated No. 69089 but never carried. Withdrawn in 1948.

No. 69108, Worsdell 0–6–2T version of class J25.

No. 9110, allocated No. 69110 but scrapped in 1948 without being renumbered. All the other locomotives of the class received their new numbers.

No. 69120, Reid 0–6–2T built for banking on the Cowlairs Incline.

No. 69136 in an odd style of painting, depicting both earlier 'British Railways' on the tank sides and the later lion-and-wheel emblem.

No. 69222, the sole engine of the class with the original type of boiler and pop safety valves on the dome. This boiler was transferred from No. 9151 in 1951.

457

No. 69252 of class N5. These engines differ only from class N4 in having Stephenson's link motion in place of Joy's valve gear, both being identical in appearance.

F. Jones

No. 69311, class N5/2, fitted with extended side tanks and the only locomotive of the class to be so treated.

458

No. 9372 (No. 69372), still carrying the old N.E.R.-type of brass safety-valve column. Most of them latterly had pop safety valves. Some of the class were superheated with extended smokeboxes, thus presenting similar differences in appearance to their tender counterparts, class J21 (page4 17).

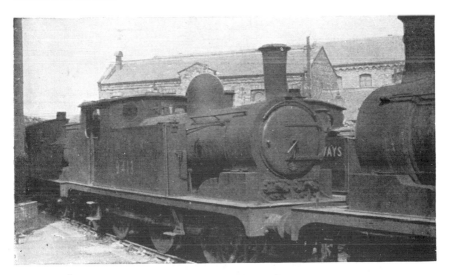

No. 9413, allocated No. 69413 but scrapped in 1950 without being renumbered. Some locomotives of class N8 were also fitted with piston valves; none of class N9 were superheated. No. 69429 carried the old brass column type of safety valve.

R. M. Casserley

No. 69430, the first of the Ivatt 5′8″ 0–6–2T's, which had longer side tanks than its successors.

No. 69468, with condensing apparatus for working through the Metropolitan tunnels. Most of the class were at first so fitted, but it was removed on many of those which later left the London area.

No. 69444, with condensing apparatus removed. Some of these engines received superheaters.

No. 9522 (69522), one of the few engines to be turned out in post-war green.

No. 69596, one of a series built without condensing gear and with longer chimneys. This locomotive retains the Ramsbottom safety valves as originally fitted; most of the class later acquired Ross pop valves.

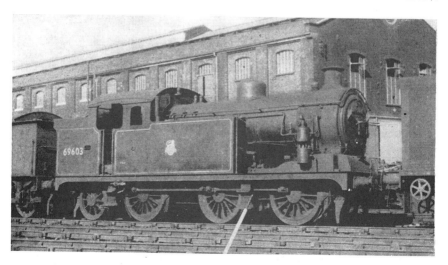

No. 69603, one of the original G.E.R. series. Originally fitted with Belpaire fireboxes, all eventually received round-topped boilers. Some of the class acquired the later style of chimney as fitted to subsequent engines of class N7 (opposite).

No. 69642, L.N.E.R. development of class N7, as first fitted with Belpaire fireboxes, but most were later converted to the round-topped variety. Some N7 engines were dual fitted, others had either vacuum or Westinghouse brakes only.

No. 69733, one of the final series, Nos. 69702–69733, which were constructed at Doncaster and built new with round-topped boilers. Nos. 69672 onwards also had the higher bunkers without coal rails.

No. E9816 (No. 69816), one of the original Robinson Great Central 4–6–2T's.

No. 69832, one of the 1925 post-grouping series, with L.N.E.R. boiler mountings.

A. F. Cook

No. 9794 (No. 69794), North Eastern 'Whitby' unsuperheated tank.

No. 69793, 'Whitby' tank with superheater. The smokebox doors on this class
varied between the two designs, as illustrated in the two comparative views of
class D20 (see pages 387–8).

No. 9778 (No. 69778), N.E.R. 4–6–2 unsuperheated shunting tank. Some of the locomotives of this class were superheated and the same variations in the boiler mountings and smokeboxes apply as in the case of class A6 (page 465).

No. 69880, N.E.R. 4–6–2T converted from 4–4–4T. All were superheated, but the domes, chimneys and smokeboxes varied amongst different engines in the same way as on classes A6 and A7. There are also three varieties of bunker as found on class G5 (see pages 427–8).

R. M. Casserley

No. 69902. One of the original G.C.R. locomotives. This engine has a Great Central-type chimney, the others carried an L.N.E.R. pattern, as in the illustration below.

No. 69904, one of the two L.N.E.R.-built ones, with altered side-tanks and side-window cabs. The rear bogie was formerly booster fitted, as were also those on Nos. 69901 and 69905. The apparatus was later removed.

No. 69922, North Eastern heavy shunting 4–8–0T. No. 69914 of this class was superheated.

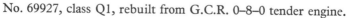

R. M. Casserley

No. 69927, class Q1, rebuilt from G.C.R. 0–8–0 tender engine.

No. 69999. Gresley 2–8–8–2T Garratt locomotive, the most powerful engine ever to run in the British Isles.

2136, Hope   Sentinel Railcar

R. M. Casserley

Sentinel Railcar No. 38, *Pearl*, which was scrapped in 1947, was one of the last survivors of these steam railcars and was similar to *Hope*, which was the only one to last into 1948.

469

BRITISH RAILWAYS STANDARD DESIGN

No. 70022 *Tornado*, 'Britannia' class.

R. J. Buckley

No. 70044, with Westinghouse brakes. No. 70043 was similarly fitted. This brake has now been removed from both engines.

No. 71000 *Duke of Gloucester*, 3-cylinder Caprotti engine, the only one of its class.

No. 72007 *Clan Mackintosh*, light 'Pacific' with 6'2" wheels.

No. 73113 *Lyonesse*, Standard Class 5 mixed-traffic 4-6-0.

No. 73139, with Caprotti valve gear, also showing the later type of tender as fitted to the more recently constructed engines of this class.

No. 75033, a lighter version of 4–6–0 with 5′8″ wheels, for intermediate passenger work. No. 75029 was fitted with a double chimney in 1958.

No. 76073, 5′3″ 2–6–0 for intermediate passenger and cross-country work.

No. 77016, a smaller design of 5′3″ passenger engine.

No. 78054, Class 2 passenger engine with 5′0″ wheels.

No. 80071, standard suburban and semi-express passenger 2-6-4T.

No. 82014, Class 3 passenger 2-6-2T.

No. 84004, light Class 2 motor fitted 2-6-2T.

No. 90732, the last engine of the series, named *Vulcan*.

No. 90774 *North British*, the last locomotive of the series.

No. 92049, standard Class 9 2-10-0.

No. 92028, with Franco-Crosti boiler.

No. 92024, with Franco-Crosti boiler replaced by orthodox type.

481

R. M. Casserley

No. 92250 fitted with Giesl ejector.

British Railways

No. 92220, *Evening Star*, the last steam locomotive built by British Railways.

Preserved locomotives

Below are lists of the principal locations at which preserved locomotives formerly in service on British Railways may be found. The key refers to the map on both end-papers.

For ease of reference, the engines at each location are shown under their B.R. numbers. These are readily found in the main text, which is in numerical order, but in many instances engines have been restored to their pre-Nationalisation or pre-grouping condition under their original numbers.

Most of these museums and sites also have other engines which were never owned by British Railways, having been taken out of service before 1948, not to mention numerous industrial and other privately owned locomotives, and even, in a few instances, engines from abroad. There are also at various other locations a considerable number of engines which are preserved privately and which are not on public view.

It should be noted that not infrequently locomotives are moved from one site to another, and in a few cases the information given may no longer apply.

Museums (M) static exhibits

M1   Science Museum, London
      4073
M2   Glasgow Museum of Transport
      57566, 62277, 62469, HR 103,
      CR 123
M3   Leicester Transport Museum
      44027, 49395, 62660, 63601
M4   Swindon Railway Museum
      2516, 3440, 4003, 9400
M5   Birmingham Science Museum
      46235
M6   Dundee City Museum
      46464
M7   Motive Power Museum, Lytham
      St Anne's, Lancashire
      68095

M8   Butlin's Holiday Camp, Minehead,
      Somerset
      32678, 46229
M9   Butlin's Holiday Camp, Pwllheli,
      Caernarvonshire
      46203
M10   Bleadon and Uphill Station,
      Somerset
      1338
M11   Tiverton Museum, Somerset
      1442

Steam centres (SC) mostly static exhibits, but engines sometimes steamed giving short rides, mostly at summer weekends

SC1   Tyseley Steam Trust, Birmingham
      4983, 7027, 7029, 7752, 7760,
      30120, 30777, 45428, 45593, 50621,
      60800, 68846
SC2   Steamtown, Carnforth, Lancashire
      5643, 6960, 35005, 44767, 44871,
      44932, 45231, 45407, 46441, 61306
SC3   G.W.R. Society, Didcot, Berkshire
      1340, 1466, 3650, 5051, 5900, 6106,
      6697, 6998, 7808, 60532
      This society also has 1363 on
      display at Bodmin, Cornwall, and
      5572 at Taunton

SC4   Ashford Steam Centre, Kent
      31065, 31263, 35028
SC5   Bressingham Hall, Diss, Norfolk
      30102, 32662, 41966, 42500, 46100,
      46233, 65567, 70013
SC6   Quainton Road, nr Aylesbury,
      Buckinghamshire
      6024, 7715, 30585, 34016, 41298,
      46447
SC7   Dinting Railway Centre, Glossop,
      Manchester
      30925, 45596, 45690, 58926

SC8 Scottish Railway Preservation
Centre, Falkirk, Stirlingshire
55189, 65243, 80105

SC9 Bulmer's Cider Railway, Hereford
5786, 6000

SC10 Stour Valley Preservation Society,
Chappell & Wake's Colne, Essex
30841

SC11 Somerset and Dorset Circle,
Radstock
53808

SC12 Haven Street, Isle of Wight
W24 (30209), 32640

SC13 Dowty Preservation Society,
Ashchurch, Gloucestershire
46201

Preserved lines (OP) fully operational, but mostly only at weekends during the summer
months

OP1 Keighley and Worth Valley
Railway, Yorkshire
5775, 30072, 34092, 41241, 41708,
42700, 43924, 45025, 45212, 48431,
51218, 51243, 51456, 52044, 68077,
69023, 69523, 75078, 80002

OP2 Severn Valley Railway,
Bridgnorth
1501, 3205, 4141, 4566, 4930, 5164,
5764, 7819, 43106, 45110, 46443,
46521, 47383, 48773 (8233), 70000,
75079, 80079

OP3 North Yorkshire Moors Railway,
Grosmont
62005, 63395, 65894

OP4 Dart Valley Railway,
Buckfastleigh, Devon
1369, 1420, 1450, 1638, 4555, 6412,
6430, 6435, 7827

OP5 Torbay Railway, Paignton (worked
by Dart Valley Railway–engines
may be changed around)
4588, 80064

OP6 Bluebell Railway, Sheffield Park,
Sussex
9017, 30064, 30096, 30583, 31027,
31178, 31323, 31592, 32473, 32636,
32655, 34023, 58850, 75027

OP7 Lakeside and Haverthwaite
Railway, Barrow-in-Furness
42073, 42085

OP8 Lochty Railway, Fife
60009

OP9 Middleton Railway, Leeds
68153

OP10 Vale of Rheidol, Aberystwyth
(narrow-gauge, worked by B.R.)
7, 8, 9

OP11 Tal-y-Llyn, Towyn, Merioneth
(narrow-gauge)
3, 4

OP12 Festiniog, Caernarvonshire
(narrow-gauge)
no B.R. locomotives

OP13 Welshpool and Llanfair
(narrow-gauge)
822, 823

Other planned preserved lines (PP) not yet operational

PP1 Main-line Steam Trust,
Loughborough
34039, 45231

PP2 Midland Railway Project Group,
Derby
47327, 47357, 47445, 47564, 73129

PP3 Tenterden Railway Company
(former Kent and East Sussex
Railway)
30065, 30070, 31556, 31618, 32650,
32670

PP4 North Norfolk Railway,
Sheringham
61572, 65462

PP5 Peterborough Locomotive Society
73050

PP6 Dean Forest Railway Preservation
Society, Lydney, Gloucestershire
5541

PP7 West Somerset Railway Company
(Taunton–Minehead)
no locomotives yet

PP8 Cranmore–Shepton Mallet
(former G.W.R. Cheddar Valley
Line)
30928, 47493, 75029, 92203

PP9 Scottish Railway Preservation
Society, Aviemore
expect to have 45025 and 46521